ALWAYS PICKED LAST

PRAISE FOR *ALWAYS PICKED LAST*

"After reading *Always Picked Last* I was eager to let people know about the book and Kevin's work. Parents, teachers, coaches: get this book and share it with your kids. I train anti-bullying and know the subject well. Nobody does it better than Kevin... nobody!" —Ken Baum, Author and trainer to the world's best athletes

"Most people are afraid to be who they are, to be open and transparent for fear of ridicule. Not Kevin. He's not afraid to put himself out there, whether in his training or sharing his story of having been bullied. I really respect that about him. He is where he is today because who he used to be drove him to this point. —Marcus Davis, UFC Veteran"

"Kevin's book was such an inspiration! I had a great time reading it to my kids. We could all relate to Kevin's story. My kids now understand they have a choice. They can let bullies bring them down and steal their happiness or they can rise above them and become whatever they want to be! A must read for any age!! Great book to read with family." —Kitty Mcafferty, Founder R.I.S.E. And Stand

"An inspirational story of a victim turned survivor through hope, faith, and discipline." —Dr. Kate Roberts, Boston based psychologist and bullying expert

"More than a memoir, *Always Picked Last* contains thoughtful, and at times philosophical, reflections on bullying, childhood, parenting, growth and personal improvement. Kearns has a strong sense of self-awareness, but also recognizes the universality of his experience, so he uses his story as a conduit for inspiration and the self-improvement of others. The message is powerful and the narrative is engaging and relatable." —Kwill Books

To John Kevin Kearns.

Although we only had a short time on this planet,
it was long enough for me to become the man I am today.

Thanks, Dad.

DISCLAIMER

This book is based on my memory of events as I recall them. To protect the privacy of the people who appear in this book, most names and identifying characteristics have been changed. I have done my best to be as candid as possible about my experiences.

Copyright 2013 Kevin Kearns
First Tambuli Edition: November 15, 2016

ISBN-13: 978-0692789094
ISBN-10: 069278909X
Library of Congress Control Number: 2016956168

Designed by Summer Bonne
Edited by Victoria Touati

ALWAYS PICKED LAST

(SECOND EDITION)

A Guide to Finding Your Way in Life and
Conquering the Bullies Along the Way

Kevin Kearns

with

Kathleen Birmingham

www.TambuliMedia.com
Spring House, PA USA

TABLE OF CONTENTS

ACKNOWLEDGMENTS

I would like to acknowledge and thank the following people for their support and encouragement during the creation of this book:

- Geoff and Peter Harvey, who helped this book come to life through their financial kindness.

- Mark Cameron for being one of my oldest and closest friends.

- Deacon Dave for sharing his story at Mass and for giving me the vision to finish this book.

- Marcus Davis for being the honorable man he is and for adding his input to this book from a FIGHTER'S perspective.

- Kathleen "Kit" Birmingham, my writer, for her talents and skills in bringing this story to life. I would especially like to credit her patience and fortitude over the past few years during our Monday evening conversations for turning my story into a book.

- My wife, Donna, and my daughters, Emily and Shannon, who gave me their love and patience during the creation of this book.

- To Lionel "Lutha" Beane, one of my oldest and dearest friends who stuck by me through high school and beyond.

- To Nick Peet and his team at Fighters Only magazine who let a C+ in high school English write 100 articles for them and designed the cover of my book.

- To Mark Wiley and Tambuli Media for taking on all my content and believing in my vision and mission.

- To Tony Rice for setting up all my talks in the UK.

- To Shihan Scott O'keefe for having my back while traveling and lecturing.

- To Kennedy Lodato, my good friend and mentor, who has always had his ear open for me.

- To my yoga teachers Jacqui Bonwell, Jordan Lashley, Masaaki Okamura, Erica Magro and alike for teaching me "it's just for now."

- To Officer Fred Leland for encouraging me to keep moving on this book.

- And to everyone else I haven't mentioned, who has inspired, encouraged, and supported me through the years, I express my most sincere thanks.

PUBLISHER'S FOREWORD

Bullying is dirty business. The cycles of what happens to create a bully, of what happens to make one susceptible to being bullied, and how these interactions lead to substance abuse and suicide later in life, are related to how children are treated and treat others, and how parents raise their children and teacher's watch over them. There's just no excuse for bullying in a humane world.

When kids complain of feeling ill, skip school, express fears about things that may otherwise seem benign, we need to ask questions. I was bullied in school and was beaten up a few times. Thankfully, my mother enrolled me in martial arts classes. My confidence in who I was, and my ability to stand my ground, changed everything. The harm that bullying creates in us often carries into adulthood. That's why it's an issue for all of us.

It was life-changing for Kevin Kearns who wasn't athletic and so was "always picked last." And sfter losing his father at a young age, Kevin felt adrift and alone, making him a perfect target for intensified bullying. His life was miserable, but through mentors, martial arts and physical training Kevin was able to gain confidence and turn it all around. Today, Coach Kevin Kearns is a hero to many school children and their parents and teachers, through his tireless anti-bullying efforts and personal coaching. And he has a body like Superman and the heart of a saint.

I've known Kevin for 20 years and it is an honor and privilege to publish his spiritually uplifting memoir and guide, *Always Picked Last*. When you read it your life will be affected in positive ways. Share that positivity forward.

Dr. Mark Wiley
Publisher, Tambuli Media

FOREWORD BY PETER TWIST

Despite greater awareness, media coverage, and intervention programs, bullying remains a real challenge for schools and in all walks of life.

The skills required to navigate bullying are not only essential for school survival, but also needed for lifelong relationships – when families move and a new circle of friends are introduced, joining a sports team, at the workplace or a relationship that no longer feels nice to be a part of. In the school yard and beyond, there are many places where bullying may appear.

The one constant in life is change – the people we find most frequently in our days will change and the new people who take their place will sometimes either be a gift or an uncomfortable challenge.

By the same token, that same constant change is what will help us when we need to improve what is being imposed on us by our environment. Taking control to achieve change, changing our mindset, changing our activities, and changing our inner circle are some of the ways to quarterback our life and improve our days.

I'm not a bullying expert. However, I have mentored thousands of kids over the past two decades in my sport training camps, and, like most people, have experienced bullying firsthand myself.

You may relate.

Bullying can sometimes take the forms of obvious and overt physical and verbal abuse. Often, though, it can be subtle and systematic. Bullying can take many forms: A persistent, unwelcomed behavior may be imposed on us as consistent criticism, social isolation, cruel rumors to damage reputations, teasing, menacing looks to intimidate, cyber bullying or social exclusion.

None of these feel good, and, it is easy to feel trapped and powerless.

From his own childhood to his present-day MMA coaching success, Kevin Kearns weaves an easy-to-read story that explains his effective approach to bullying and making positive change happen. For example, he suggests finding someone to help expand your world so you don't get caught up in an endless, inescapable loop, and also recommends finding something you're really good at while surrounding yourself with others of the same mindset. Along the same lines, Kearns encourages readers to make a powerful difference in their own lives by spending more time with those who share similar interests, and are equally passionate about becoming their personal best. These types of choices not only make us feel differently about ourselves, they change the types of interactions we experience daily.

One of my favorite philosophical sayings is, "Great Spirits have always encountered violent opposition from mediocre minds." I interpret this not as a comment on intelligence, but rather as an enthusiastic spirit who expresses a different way to think, embraces new ideas, and perhaps demonstrates a different attitude than some around them, often despite disdain and putdowns.

Our world seems to feel safe and less threatened when everyone acts and thinks the "same." But not everyone is the same, especially those who are most special. I think the author of the previous quote, Albert Einstein, created this statement when he himself experienced bullying firsthand. As he created and proposed new, exciting concepts and theories, Einstein faced aggressive putdown from more limited thinkers, who were most likely intimidated or simply didn't "get" his approach. They attempted to shut him down and shut him out, yet his spirit prevailed.

In my past work of cultivating contrarian athletic exercise methods, and suggesting alternative ways to see the world and live in it, I have always had an unapologetically enthusiastic spirit while enjoying a tremendous following of like-minded people who were inspired by what I shared. At the same time, there was a small number who violently opposed who I am, my spirit, my attitude, and my ideas. What attracts and motivates 99%, also seems to alienate and repel the 1%.

Do not get knocked off your path. Do not stop being your special self, because of the smallest percent who spews the ugliest voice. They usually have ulterior motives or are not solid enough to receive new ideas and information without conflict.

I believe in creating, defining, and following my own path, and, highly encourage you to do the same. We all want to fit in, be accepted, and feel good among our peers. But, just fitting in is an intolerable option if we do not feel aligned with those who make up our inner circle of like-minded people. The time to fit in is when it is the right fit for the right reasons. Because you share interests and are passionate about the same things, your attitudes are similar, and you have mutual respect to things and ideas that appear "new" or "different."

To mitigate the impact of the most intense bullying, reach out and find help while you discover something you truly enjoy and become very good at. This involvement builds your self-esteem, and enables you to form nurturing friendships with people who share your specific interests.

I am a huge believer in giving good energy. People either give energy or suck energy. Bullying is the peak of energy suckers. Bullying can negatively affect our mind, heart, and spirit. When we thrive on self-assurance, it creates self-doubt. One cannot overstate the upside to shifting our personal daily landscape to doing the things we love with people who transfer contagious enthusiasm as you interact together in and around your core passions.

As a coach of over 700 pro athletes and operating Twist gyms in several countries, I might seem biased towards the role of fitness as part of your strategy to bullying. I am. But it is not bias, it is certainty. Improving your body's strength and fitness transfers similar feelings of strength and fitness to mind and spirit. It is therapeutic and the positive outcomes translate to personal pride which buoys confidence and self-esteem.

As you engage in a fitness program, you will find yourself spending more time with people who work on their strength and fitness, and are striving to become stronger inside by working on themselves – as opposed to the bully. The bully strives to gain fake power by stealing energy from others because he or she does not feel strong inside and is not yet capable of acting with grace, humility, compassion and respect. Shifting part of your days to healthy pursuits such as strength and fitness will bring new conversations with people who will share their encouragement and acknowledgement of your progression.

The path to not letting others knock you off track and ultimately unlock your true potential begins with knowledge. Understanding what contributes to a culture of bullying and why an individual imposes behavior that makes us feel diminished is important information to regain our mindset and confidence. Putting Coach Kearns's advice into action will help you be your best, be more certain of what you deserve, become better aware of the steps you can take to change your world, and, ultimately, own the process.

As a top pro coach, Kevin Kearns not only knows how to coach you to create change in yourself and your environment, he also can relate with genuine compassion because he has been on the receiving end of relentless bullying, which caused him to question himself and his worth.

Always Picked Last unveils his amazing and inspirational journey to the mindset and action steps you need to make a difference in your life and to help shape the people and situations you experience.

I encourage you to always be courageous in your simple but honorable pursuit to "Be Yourself" and "Become Your Best." Getting back on track, when others derail us, takes courage, but, with Coach Kearns' plan you can do it with purpose and make sure you define your own path, which is custom made for you. It's only when you work through tough changes that you become freer to enjoy the process surrounded by good energy.

Peter Twist
President & CEO, Twist Sport Conditioning Inc.
11 year NHL Coach

CHAPTER 1

"Come on, Kevin!" shouted Tony. "Just jump over it!"

I looked at the oscillating sprinkler. My best friend, Tony, and our other neighbor, Dave, stood on the far side of the sprinkler, big grins on their faces, their shorts a damp testament to their bravery.

At the ripe old age of almost nine, I knew that I had to overcome my reluctance to try something new. But this wasn't just about jumping

Friends or enemies?

over a sprinkler... they had a hold of the hose and were wiggling it, moving it, so that it wasn't a stationary target.

This was a set up for a letdown.

Most of the time, I failed at whatever activity my buddies came up with. But this was just jumping over a dumb sprinkler. Moving or not, I knew that if I didn't pass this test, it was going to be a long, lonely summer.

Just then, Toni's little sister burst out from the house in her bright pink and orange sun-suit and without hesitation ran directly in front of me and did a little hop over the sprinkler and took her place beside my friends, her grin mirroring theirs.

Great... shown up by a little girl. Tony had stopped moving it when his sister showed up, but she didn't know that.

The idea here is to time the movement of the sprinkler and watch carefully to see which way the hose was moving with your jump. I'm not very good at timing, but chanted to myself, "It's just water, it's just water, it's just water."

Closing my eyes (I know, not the greatest idea), I charged at the sprinkler just as it turned its rays of water in my direction, surprising me. I gasped in reaction to the frigid water and instantly choked as water filled my mouth and sprayed up my nose.

I opened my eyes, just in time, to avoid tripping over the sprinkler, and made an uncoordinated one-legged, hop jump and then ran over to where my friends stood.

Well, I'd done it.

They exchanged a look.

Not just any look.

That look.

The one that says, "See, he can't even jump over a sprinkler without being a moron."

Just ignore them, I kept saying to myself.

I forced a smile and said, "Let's do it again!"

And this time, I managed to time it just right, more by accident than anything else, and my moment of failure was over.

Summertime, in my little neighborhood had few opportunities. So Tony and Dave made up my world. We were like the three Musketeers and I liked the feeling of belonging. Who doesn't?

We chased each other around the yard, jumping through the sprinkler, slipping on the wet grass and loving every second of our first day of summer vacation.

Once school lets out, summer stretched before us like a highway to anywhere. It didn't matter where we would go. All that mattered was that we were on it and headed somewhere.

Everett, Massachusetts has amazing summers. The sky's brilliant blue peeking through the deep green of the huge old elm trees that grew tall, dark and black, silhouetted against the sunlit sky. The just cool air with the promise of greater heat later, and the smell of freshly cut grass was my favorite fragrance.

We stopped frolicking in the water and were on our backs underneath the great trees in Tony's yard.

The back screen door of the Capitani's house screeched opened and Mrs. Capitani called, "Kevin! Your mother didn't know you were here."

At that, Tony and Dave pushed themselves up on their elbows, exchanged another one of those looks and immediately started mimicking what my mother might have said on the phone, using high-pitched voices.

"Oh, Kevin, be careful crossing the street."

"Do you want me to walk you to Tony's house? It's pretty far to go on your own."

"Want me to hold your hand, Kevie?"

I glared at them, standing up for myself, "I've been crossing the street by myself for years!"

This much was true, and until I was seven or eight it was usually when old Mr. Birch was standing there in his orange vest and hand-held STOP sign, doing his volunteer duty as the traffic guard for the elementary school kids crossing Dartmouth Street.

My mother would let me cross alone while she watched from the window, knowing that Mr. Birch, who I got to know in first grade, was there to stop any of the infrequent traffic if necessary.

"Your mom says it's OK for you to stay for lunch," Mrs. Capitani said, her voice loud enough to be heard throughout the neighborhood announced, and I winced at the volume.

Now the whole neighborhood would know what I was doing.

"Ooohhh… Kevie's staying for lunch," taunted Dave. I wanted to sock him in the nose, but he was pretty big for his age. Instead I reached down and with my hand tossed a handful of water from the grass up into the air and before another taunt could be launched, another game had started.

We made up games all the time, inventing rules as necessary. This time, Tony and Dave decided that if you hit someone in the face with the handful of water, you get a point.

What they didn't really do was decide if we were teams or if we were playing every man for himself. Tony's little sister tired of the game and went inside leaving me the sole target for both boys. Fortunately, because I'm so small, I'm also quick; so it took a while for both Tony and Dave to get enough points to win.

Twenty-one.

We always play games until we reach the goal of twenty-one.

It's like some kind of magic number.

Fortunately, Tony and Dave were arguing about who won first. This time their hostility was directed at each other rather than at me and I sat panting in the sun, enjoying my moment of peace.

"Hey guys! Let's play follow the leader. You have to do what I do." With that bold announcement, bold for me anyway, I started hopping like I was in a sack race and hopped over the sprinkler.

Competition is the name of the game for my friends and me.

The fight forgotten, Tony and Dave obediently hopped through the sprinkler. Then, because I didn't have any better ideas, I said, "OK, Tony, you be the leader."

And off it went from there.

I managed to avoid being the leader more than a couple of times, and because my two friends had such a drive to compete, they didn't really notice.

Mission accomplished.

I learned that by blending into the background, I was able to enjoy playing with my friends without too much notice being taken of me. And when they didn't notice me, we got along pretty well, which means they didn't pick on me. Well, not much anyway.

But eventually, that spotlight always found me. When it did, I knew I wasn't going to like it.

"Hey, Dave! Can you do this?" Tony launched himself onto his hands and "walked" a couple of steps on his hands.

"Sure I can." Dave managed to overshoot his balance and landed up on his back.

Tony and I both burst out laughing.

Dave wasn't usually the butt of the joke, so to me, this was especially funny.

He rolled over, hopped to his feet, muttering, "I'll show ya."

Again.

And again.

And yet again.

Dave failed every time. Each time I heard him land on his back, a puff of air forced out of his chest cavity with an audible grunt, and I winced.

I knew I wasn't going to like what happened next. I also had no way to stop it.

Dave faced me and challenged, "YOU do it, then, smart ass."

I gulped.

My heart dropped like a stone, my stomach contracting in fear.

"Yeah, Kev. Show us how it's done!"

"You chicken?"

"Fraidy cat!"

Using the emotional momentum from having enjoyed the past hour and a half with my friends, I threw myself forward as I'd seen Tony do, and, just like Dave, I overshot my mark and landed hard on my back.

Only, I didn't land on the grass.

The strange crunching sound coincided with the pain in my back and the water that seemed to be coming from every direction.

I couldn't breathe.

My eyes closed to protect them from the spray of water, and my imagination went into overdrive.

Maybe I'd broken my back!

What if I could never walk again?

I half expected Tony to come over and help me up.

Instead, I heard a howl of anger and then felt the sprinkler being jerked out from underneath me.

"Kevin, ya dork! You broke it!"

"Now what are we gonna do?"

"You are such a loser!"

I peeked out through one eye and saw Tony and Dave trying to re-adjust the sprinkler, but the huge fountain of water coming from the edge where the hose connected told me I'd broken the connection.

Dave tried to yank the mess out of Tony's hands, and Tony kept turning around, keeping his back to Dave as he tried to block the water enough to see the damage.

"Let me see!" Dave demanded, grabbing the far edge of the sprinkler.

"NO!" Tony shouted.

A peculiar tug of war commenced between the two boys.

I could have predicted what happened next.

Yanking hard, Dave landed on his backside with the now empty sprinkler in his hands and Tony danced away, using his thumb to spray Dave and me.

I was still trying to figure out if my back was broken, but no one paid me any attention. I rolled over onto my front and gingerly pushed myself up to a standing position.

By now Tony and Dave were right up against the house and Mrs. Capitani's entrance onto the scene was announced by the screech of the back door.

In his frenzy, Tony didn't hear it, and he swung around, the spray of the hose following him.

It all seemed to happen in slow motion.

One second he was whooping and hollering. The next second, the full force of the water coming from the hose was trained on Mrs. Capitani and he drenched his mother from head to toe.

All sounds of laughter and gaiety stopped.

Dripping, and as angry as I have ever seen her, Mrs. Capitani flew down the steps, marched over to the faucet, and, with a vicious twist, turned off the water.

"No more water today."

None of us dared to challenge that statement.

I figured Tony was lucky she didn't haul off and smack him. If it had been his dad, things would have turned physical and ugly in seconds.

Silence fell over the yard as we watched Tony's mom march back up the steps to the house.

After the next screech of the screen door closing behind Mrs. Capitani's indignant back, we all exchanged wide-eyed looks.

But that didn't last for long.

Once Mrs. Capitani was out of sight, Dave ran over and grabbed the hose out of Tony's hands. He laughed and taunted Tony as he pranced just out of Tony's reach.

An empty hose didn't seem like much of a game to me, but Dave had other ideas.

"Watch this!"

"Hey, look out!" This from Tony as he danced back away from Dave who was twirling around and around, the hose extending out from his hands at waist level.

Tony wasn't quick enough.

Smack!

The sound of the hose hitting Tony's stomach sickened me.

Dave froze.

If it had happened to me, Tony and Dave would have just ganged up on me and laughed.

But this time, Dave hit Tony.

Tony's eyes blazed. He leaped to his feet and charged at Dave.

Dave dropped the hose and ran.

Within seconds, Tony caught up to Dave and, with a closed fist, smacked him high on his shoulder. I could see Dave's skin first turn white at the site of the impact and then an angry red.

The red blotch stood out against Dave's white skin like an ink stain.

All this time, I stood, rooted in place.

Tony looked in my direction and when our eyes met, I could see he was still really angry.

Somehow I didn't know what to do.

Apologize?

But it wasn't my fault.

He turned away from Dave and picked up the hose. This time, when he started swinging it, he raised it high over his head.

"Hey, look at me. I'm a cowboy!"

For a second, I watched, wishing I could do that, just go from a moment of anger to the next moment of joy.

Then Tony's eyes fell on me again.

"Kevin's one of my cattle. I'm gonna rope him."

With that, Tony let loose of the hose and the hard end of the hose hit my jaw. There had been no time to react. The force of the blow knocked me from my feet.

I sat there, stunned, holding my hand to my jaw.

"Ya gonna cry?"

"Go ahead and cry…be a cry baby!"

Taunting voices echoed in my ears as I got to my feet once more.

Only this time, I didn't have any ideas.

I didn't know how to pretend it didn't happen.

The atmosphere in Tony's backyard had turned dark and ugly.

I wanted like anything to keep playing with Tony, but I didn't like being the brunt of their jokes.

I didn't like being hurt.

The games they played always seemed to hurt someone… usually me.

With their jeering voices still echoing in my ears, I half-ran from Tony's back yard to the sidewalk out front.

Were they following me?

Part of me hoped they were.

What I really wanted was for them to beg me to come back.

I waited for another moment.

My best friend for as long as I could remember had hurt me.

And then laughed about it.

So far, neither boy showed any sign of coming after me. I could hear their shouts from the backyard. Apparently, a new game had begun without me.

Holding back the hot tears of humiliation and betrayal, I started the lonely journey home.

One house.

Two houses.

The school.

As I trudged up the street, I looked at Dartmouth Elementary school, directly across the street from my house, looking sad, lonely, and empty.

Just how I felt.

Its windows stared blankly at me as I plodded home. I'd made a jeering face at the school when I'd set out this morning, crossing the street and heading to Tony's house without Mom knowing, although, she always knew where I was. Where else would I go?

This morning seemed so far away now, and I didn't feel nearly as confident as I had then.

I didn't like the twisted sick feeling in my stomach.

I rubbed both my jaw and my stomach.

Maybe I deserved this feeling.

I had decided to go to Tony's house without permission.

I had crossed the street alone.

Maybe this is what I get for being so sneaky.

Now, I kinda wished I could go to school today. At least at school I had someone to play with.

It was usually Tony.

But at school he was nicer than he had been today.

We were friends. Best friends. We'd been best friends since before I could remember.

I knew that.

I also knew Tony only showed off when he's trying to impress Dave.

I just wished he hadn't laughed so hard when the hose hit me. I could still hear the loud smack right next to my ear as it collided with my jaw.

As I had done just a couple hours before when I started out for Tony's house, I looked both ways before crossing Dartmouth Street there in front of my house and then climbed the two steps up to my front porch and went inside.

"Kevin! What are you doing home so soon? I thought you were having lunch at Tony's." My mom looked up from her ironing in surprise.

I mumbled something about watching television.

"No," she said, "you don't want to watch television now. It's a beautiful day outside. Enjoy the sunshine and fresh air while you can."

Mom hadn't even barely looked at me after her quick glance of surprise when I'd dragged my feet through the front door.

I flopped into my dad's chair. "Tony hit me with the hose."

"Oh?" Moms are good at injecting a lot of meaning into a single word. She kept ironing, but I sensed she was listening a little more carefully now.

"Dave hit Tony first, so Tony punched him. Then, Tony started swinging the hose like some kind of cowboy or something and it hit me right here." I pointed to the now swollen part of my jaw.

I pushed on it to make it hurt again.

I needed her to listen to me.

To believe me.

I needed her to help me figure out why my best friend had just hurt me.

"Honey, you know that boys will be boys. I'm sure he didn't mean it." She hung up Dad's shirt she had just finished ironing, reached into the laundry basket, shook out the next one, and then started ironing again without so much as a glance at me. "You'll see, tomorrow you'll both just forget all about it and be good friends again."

As much as I wanted to believe her, the ache in my stomach told me I wasn't so sure.

I brought my knees up to my chest, snuggled down deeper into Dad's chair, wishing it was Saturday. If it were Saturday, we would both sit in this chair and watch *Creature, Double Feature* like we always did.

Summer started looking a little long.

*   *   *   *   *

The next morning my mom poked her head around the door just as I woke up.

"Wake up, Sleepyhead. Tony's mom is taking you two to the beach today so get up and get ready."

It didn't take me but a couple seconds to process what she said.

The beach!

It wasn't so much that it was a bus ride that excited me, but the fact that our destination was the beach. Summer days languished like a great yellow-white void where the minutes turn into hours unless something exciting happens.

Like going to the beach.

With Tony.

Without Dave.

Tony's mom was taking us. She and my mom took turns going to either the beach or the pool. The beach was my favorite because Dave never came; he could only go to the pool.

Ten cents was the price of freedom. Ten cents and the twenty-five minutes it took to get there. Twenty-five minutes where I sat with my face glued to the window, desperate to catch my first glimpse of the ocean, and to keep myself from getting carsick... if you can get carsick in a bus.

There it was.

I lifted my face and sniffed. I could always smell it before I saw it. There is no mistaking the sea-salted air, the way my skin felt moist but not wet.

One more turn, then the diamond glitters made me squint and turn my head away, just long enough to adjust to the dancing scattered sunlight.

Tony and I were both bouncing on the balls of our feet in impatience, hoisting ourselves down the aisle, one hand on a seatback on each side as we waited our turn to get off the bus. We had our towels and sandals. Who needed a beach chair? We had no intention of spending anytime on the beach.

We were going to be *in* the water.

Finally, a break appeared in the wall of people, our heads barely above their waists, and the second Tony saw an opening, he bolted.

I was right on his heels.

Shouting like warriors, we tossed our sandals and towels in a heap just before the wet edge of the sand. Not stopping, we plowed into the water, gasping at its chill. But neither one of us would show weakness to the other. If he could stand the freezing water, so could I.

This was the one time I was Tony's equal.

And one thing I could do was swim like a fish.

Whooping and splashing, we fought the tug of the undertow, trying to run with our bodies underwater and looking silly while doing it.

"You look like you're running in slow motion!"

I tried harder.

I always did around Tony. As I pushed through the water, I lost my footing and fell face first into the water and then emerged gasping.

When I broke surface, Tony was laughing at me like he always did.

But I didn't let it bug me this time. It was just the two of us in the water and he always knew his dominance over me.

When no one else was around, he had little to prove.

He'd dunk my head under water a time or two, just to make sure I knew.

I knew.

This, too, was the price to pay to go to the beach.

Most of the time, I felt like we were friends when we were at the beach.

A quick sprint up the boardwalk for a corndog or a Coke wolfed down quickly so that by the time we reached the water again, we could splash right back in.

That night I went to bed without a bath. I wanted to smell the sea in my hair, feel the grit of the sand on the sheets.

I wanted to feel alive.

And equal.

And wanted.

CHAPTER 2

I turned nine on Wednesday.

Because Dad worked, Mom got a cake from Elm Street bakery.

Tony and Dave and a couple of other neighborhood kids came over for lunch and had birthday cake afterward. As usual, we played a funny game of baseball that later became pretty famous in our neighborhood.

Directly across Dartmouth Street stood Webster Elementary School, and there we trooped with our pimple ball. We used to try to make this game work with a Wiffle ball, but it was too light. Every one of my friends in the neighborhood had their specially stuffed bat. It was just a plastic bat that came with the Wiffle ball set. Tony and Dave were the first to figure out if they cut the cap off the top of the bat and then stuff rolled newspapers into the body of the bat, you could really send the ball sailing.

I stood there waiting for the teams to be chosen.

This was the part I hated the most, but I was pretty jazzed about my new Wiffle ball bat. Mom had given it to me right before we cut the cake, so I knew we would be playing ball in the schoolyard afterward.

Tony started the team lineup. "I choose Dave!"

Naturally.

Anytime Dave was around, Tony chose him.

I really wish he didn't come.

I had tried to talk my mother out of inviting Dave to my birthday celebration that morning over breakfast.

"Mom, can we just invite Tony today and not Dave?"

She looked up from her coffee and newspaper, tilted her head to the side and said, "Now Kevin, why would you want to do that? You know that isn't nice. He'll feel left out."

Bam!

Right there she had me.

Deep inside, I really didn't want to invite Dave. Things just had a way of going sour when Dave joined our group of friends.

But, to be nice, I agreed.

Now, standing on the freshly coated blacktop that was the schoolyard, I could see Dave and Tony whispering together and laughing.

It didn't take a genius to know that they were laughing at me. I was the only one left to be chosen and it was Tony's turn to pick.

Great, last pick.

"OK, fine, we'll take Kevin."

"Yeah, but it's like having no one on the team." Dave's hard eyes let me know he wasn't joking.

"Hey, it's Kevin's birthday, have him first up to bat."

My stomach just clenched at this. I never was able to hit the ball. But, maybe this time, with my new Wiffle ball bat I would hit the ball.

"Strike one!"

"Strike two!"

"Strike three! You're out!"

Typical.

I turned away from the plate, swinging my bat, pretending that I didn't care. I had to pretend because if I didn't, the sick, hot feeling inside me would just burst through and the last thing I wanted to do was to cry in front of my friends.

Dave punched me hard in the shoulder. "Kevin, you suck at this. Why do you even keep playing?"

I jerked away from Dave and stood apart from the game, watching now as Tony got up to bat. His loaded bat looked sturdy and menacing in his hands. He held it high over his shoulders and goaded the pitcher.

"Come on, throw me a decent pitch if you can."

It never failed, the pitch was perfect, and Tony's swing even more so.

Smack!

And the ball popped into the air, past the center line, then over the fence.

"Home run!" Tony and Dave crowed.

"At least that made up for Kevin's opening strike out."

The words were muttered just loud enough for me to hear. But I wasn't going to give them the satisfaction of seeing me quit. The next time I was up to bat, I managed to connect with the ball, but because my bat wasn't weighted yet, there was no force behind my hit. The ball grounded, and didn't get past the midline of the field.

"You're out!" I went back to wait again.

Again Dave turned to me, "Man, Kevin, you really suck at this game." Then he shouted at Tony, "Why'd ya even pick him? It's a waste of time."

The boys on the other team joined in the jeering. "We didn't want him either."

"It just makes it fair. Without Kevin you two would never get any outs."

"He can't play ball."

"Loser."

They laughed and jeered and jabbed me with hands and bats and words. Still, I wouldn't give them the satisfaction of letting them know they were getting to me.

"Just wait until I get some weight in this bat. I'll show you then."

"Yeah, right. Like that's going to make any difference."

Of course it would make a difference. If I'd had a weighted bat, I was sure my ball would have at least let me get onto first base. I just knew that one day it would click.

At night I would dream of getting up to the plate, swinging and hitting the ball clear over the fence into Little Mr. Sicily's raspberry patch. It would happen one day.

I just had to keep trying.

These guys in the neighborhood, they were the only people I knew.

This was my world. Without them, there would be no one to play with.

Besides, Tony was my best friend and I just wanted to be part of something.

So when it was my turn at bat again, I kept telling myself that this was the price to pay to be able to play with the kids in the neighborhood.

You guessed it.

I struck out.

Again.

That night, Dad asked, "So, how'd the new bat work?"

"OK."

"How'd the game go? Did you get a hit?"

"Yeah. I just need to weight the bat so the next time I can hit the ball right."

"Then, let's get some newspapers." Dad and I spent the next hour tightly rolling newspapers, stuffing them into my bat, and when I was satisfied, taped the cap of the bat shut.

Next time I was really going to show the guys how well I could play ball.

I did wish, however, that my dad would go outside and just show me how to be a better athlete. I often saw Dave and his dad playing catch outside.

But I didn't like how much Mr. Braden yelled at his son. I always wondered how Dave was able to take it.

※ ※ ※ ※ ※

While my birthday had been on Wednesday, we were going to go out and celebrate as a family on Saturday. We didn't get to go out very often, so birthdays were pretty special events.

I'd chosen to go to the Brown Jug Pizza Parlor on Revere Beach Parkway.

A family favorite.

Dad opened the door and the smell of hot brick oven pizza greeted me as I rushed in. The noise, cigar and cigarette smoke, multi-colored neon lights from beer signs hanging high on the walls above dartboards, scoreboards, and sports posters and pictures greeted me as I entered.

While I didn't like the smell of the smoke, Dad loved coming here because he could have a cigar and a Schlitz without my mom nagging him about it.

Even though she was six years older than me, my sister, Jeanne, and I still fought over who got to sit next to the window on the high-backed, brown bench. They felt a little like church pews, but the atmosphere was anything but church-like.

As Mom and Dad ordered, I basked in the atmosphere of the Brown Jug. I fingered the orange and brown woven tablecloth that hung over the sides of the table. It was protected from spills on the top by a piece of glass, but I couldn't help weaving my fingers into the section of cloth that hung over the table. This I did over and over again.

I wanted to permanently etch this moment into my memory.

This was happiness. The sounds of laughing, talking, and cheering. The clink of glasses, forks, and plates. The warm feeling of almost being hugged by the atmosphere of the restaurant.

"Here you go, young man." The server handed me a Coke, another very special treat. "I hear it's your birthday!"

I couldn't keep the grin from spreading across my face. "Yep."

I didn't know what else to say.

"Well, Happy Birthday!"

There we were: the four of us.

Jeanne and I had our Cokes. Dad had his Schlitz, and, for once, Mom joined him in a beer. Usually, she drank water or iced tea.

Dad picked up his glass and said, "Well, Happy Birthday, Kevin!" We all clinked glasses, making me feel very grown up and then I sneezed at the bubbles in my nose.

I'm not quite sure when I knew I was adopted.

It wasn't something my parents ever kept a secret from me.

What I did know was that my dad really wanted a son, and, when he found out they were getting a boy, Mom said he could hardly contain himself. I looked closely at my dad as he sat across the table from me, laughing at something Mom had said. He looked like an ordinary guy from the neighborhood. His dark hair, going gray, was combed neatly, looking a little like pictures I'd seen of President Kennedy. He looked a little older than his forty-two years.

The other dads in the neighborhood didn't have any gray hair yet.

Mom had told me that my birth mother was nineteen and couldn't take care of me. There was no knowledge of my birth father.

I never thought of anyone being my father other than my dad.

I am Kevin John Kearns...my dad, John Kevin Kearns, loved me totally.

His name was John Kevin Kearns, and they named me Kevin John Kearns. I never wanted to be a part of any other family than the one I had right now.

Our server brought our pizza and set it down in the middle of the table with a flourish. "And which slice do you want, birthday boy?"

Ah, a hot, steaming cheese pizza, and right there in front of me was a piece that had a huge bubble that had popped up, browning the cheese to a crunchy golden brown. I pointed to that piece.

Jeanne protested, "Hey, I wanted that piece!"

"But it's Kevin's birthday, he gets whatever piece he wants."

I leaned over my plate, closed my eyes, and inhaled the aroma of the hot crust, the browned cheese, and made my birthday wish.

I wish life could just stay like this; it's perfect.

I knew it was time to go when the pizza was gone, but the memory of that evening would stay with me forever.

Only Mom and Dad weren't done.

Dad turned on the television to ABC. "Aha! Just in time for Lawrence Welk," and he winked at Jeanne and me and then put out a hand to Mom in invitation.

You know how you try to pretend you don't want to see your parents being affectionate, and yet when they are, there's something inside of you that goes soft and gooey, kind of like a perfectly toasted marshmallow?

That's how I felt as soon as I heard the accordion music and saw the bubbles rising up from the stage on the one color television set we had in the living room.

This was the one night of the week when Dad wouldn't be sitting in his easy chair and mom wouldn't be reclining in her rocker, the two separated by a reading lamp.

Watching from our seats on the floor, Jeanne and I both rolled our eyes and made faces, but we knew that for a few moments, Mom and Dad weren't thinking about us.

Once the big band leader himself, Lawrence Welk, announced the start of his musical variety show with his iconic, "A one-a, an' a two-a…"

Mom and Dad were transported to a time gone by.

Myron Floren on accordion, Champagne Lady Norma Zimmer, Irish tenor Joe Feeney, and Bobby Burgess and his dance partner, Cissy King, joined all of us in our small, dark living room, the ugly wallpaper with the golden and olive flowers faded into the background.

As soon as the music started, Dad reached a gallant arm toward my mom, and, with a big smile, she twirled into his arms.

Looking into each other's eyes, they danced.

Right there in the living room, they moved gracefully, despite the tight quarters of our first floor, three-family home on Dartmouth Street.

Jeanne and I continued to pretend to be disgusted, making retching sounds and rolling our eyes. But deep inside, I knew my parents loved each other very much. I smiled at the picture they made. Anyone looking in the window would see a middle-aged couple, slightly overweight, moving across the floor like it was the Ritz.

Even as we continued to poke fun at them, I knew I was loved very, very much.

※　※　※　※　※

Once my birthday was over, summer flew by in a flurry of daily activities. Either Revere Beach or the municipal pool with Mom or Mrs. Capitani was a weekly activity; although, now that I was nine, my mom and Mrs. Capitani were more and more willing to let Tony and I head over to the pool alone. The other days were spent playing ball over at Webster schoolyard across the street, jumping through the sprinklers at Tony's house because his back yard was bigger than ours or playing superheroes with our Big Jim action heroes.

Before I knew it, it was time for school to start.

I was such a cute kid!

I was now a 4th grader.

It felt pretty good to be moving up a grade.

Tony and I had talked about the beginning of school for the last week. We met on the sidewalk in front of my house before we walked to the back of the school where we had played hundreds of games of Wiffle Bat ball. This would be our last year at Webster before we moved up to the junior high school.

"Who do you suppose we got for a teacher?"

I shrugged.

I didn't really care.

For the most part, I liked the teachers at Webster. And since my mom had gotten a job as secretary to the truant officer of our school, I never wanted to make waves.

"I hear Mrs. Wallace assigns a lot of homework." Tony never was a big one for doing homework. He'd prefer to be outside hitting a ball. As if he read my mind, Tony pretended he had a bat in his hands, squinted his eyes at the imaginary ball, and with perfect form, swung. Even though he was just pretending, I could see the exact moment Tony hit the ball and knew he saw it sailing over the fence.

"Mrs. Wallace is OK. I kinda hope we get Miss Daily."

Tony wolf-whistled. "That'd be OK…she's pretty hot."

Whenever Tony talked about girls this way, I felt uncomfortable.

Yeah, sure, they are pretty nice to look at, but the last thing I wanted to do was share my feelings about our teachers with Tony. The minute he wanted to get me, he'd just turn around and embarrass me with it.

At that moment, a student who looked like he was already in junior high came up to us.

"Hey guys." He punched Tony in the shoulder.

Tony punched him back. "Hey yourself, Derek."

I gave Derek a brief smile.

I didn't want Tony to know that Derek and I had begun hanging out together after we discovered our mutual love of model building. Tony was a "man of action" and didn't have the patience to build model airplanes or tanks the way Derek and I liked to do.

Even though he stood head and shoulders above everyone else in the schoolyard, Derek looked like he didn't feel comfortable in his skin. He constantly shifted his weight from one foot to the other, and his pale blue eyes looked around, landing on one thing and then another.

When he was like this, he made me nervous.

When he was concentrating on gluing the tiny plastic model pieces together, he was like a totally different kid. He didn't seem so big and intimidating to me. Now, he just towered over me, and anyone who towers over me makes me nervous, which is just about everyone.

Once the bell rang, we trooped into the school and found our classrooms.

Derek and I were with Miss Daily.

Tony got Mrs. Wallace.

It turns out Dave was in Mrs. Wallace's class as well.

As I sat down in my desk, I was surprised that I felt somewhat relieved that Tony and I weren't in the same class. I wondered what it might be like if Derek and I could become best friends the way Tony and I used to be.

Miss Daily interrupted my thoughts by introducing herself.

A new school year had begun.

※　※　※　※　※

Three weeks into school while we were outside on the blacktop playground behind Webster school, Tony started hollering.

"What's wrong?"

Tony never screamed. He'd die before he showed fear or pain.

"I got stung by a bee!"

I ran as fast as I could to tell the playground monitor who called Tony over, and, after inspecting the bee sting, sent him to the school nurse.

After recess, I couldn't concentrate on Miss Daily's lesson of Silas Marner. It was only when I realized the whole class had started giggling that she had called on me more than once when.

"Kevin, you're daydreaming."

"No, ma'am."

Really, I wasn't daydreaming. I was worried.

What if Tony died?

I knew people could die of a bee sting.

"Do you remember the question?"

"No, ma'am."

Normally, I participated in class only if I had to, which meant I never volunteered to talk unless I was called on. This time, I ignored the impatient look she had on her face and blurted out, "Have you heard how Tony's doing?"

Now she looked puzzled.

"Tony. My friend, Tony Capitani. He got stung by a bee."

"You're worried about a little bee sting? Or are you just worried that you won't have anyone to play Big Jim with after school today?"

I don't know how word of our afternoons of playing Big Jim got around, but I wanted to melt into the floor when she said that.

Everyone in the room was listening.

That included Derek.

I didn't want to see his reaction; he might get angry at me if he knew I was still play with Tony sometimes after school.

After a small laugh, Miss Daily went on with the lesson, calling on someone else, looking for another victim after she'd humiliated me in front of everyone. Didn't she know that a bee sting was the worst thing that could happen to a kid?

Slumping in my desk, I let the rest of the school day pass me by.

I was worried about Tony.

I was hurt that Miss Daily made fun of Tony and me as we played with our action figures after school. She made it sound like we were playing with Barbies or something.

I would have traded her for Mrs. Webster any day.

As soon as the bell rang signaling the end of the day, I charged out of the room and ran over to Mrs. Webster's classroom. By the time I got there; it was empty. Mrs. Webster looked up from her desk, her eyes open in question.

"Is Tony OK?"

"Of course, Kevin, he's just fine. He left with everyone else when the bell rang."

"Thanks."

My dad's chair became a source of comfort after he passed.

I ran toward the front doors of the school. As I reached the sidewalk I could see Tony and Dave walking with Derek. They had stayed on Tony's side of the street, so all three were heading to Tony's house.

I stopped, not sure what to do.

While I was relieved that Tony was OK, I didn't want to tell Tony what Miss Daily had said, but I was pretty sure Derek would probably tell him.

Dejected, I crossed the street, trudged up the three steps to our three-family home, and let myself into the house.

Big Jim was waiting on the chest where Tony and I usually play.

I knocked him over.

Then I turned on the television and curled up in Dad's faded easy chair.

I don't know what was worse. Coming home to an empty house because my mom wasn't home yet or trying to insert myself into the group of boys heading to Tony's house.

After my humiliation in Miss Daily's classroom, I just wanted to be alone and think things through. I'd rushed to Tony's aid after he got stung. I expected to feel a little better about it than I did. Playing Big Jim with Tony always made me feel bigger than myself, more powerful and able to take on battles than in the real world I'd hide from. When I play Big Jim, I felt like I could lead the world from right to wrong.

Without Big Jim, I felt exactly like a kid.

Small.

Powerless.

Just an observer of the world.

※　※　※　※　※

Right before Thanksgiving, I saw Mrs. Blila in the hallway at school.

She had been my first grade teacher three years ago.

"Kevin, how's your dad doing?"

"He's doing pretty good."

"I'm glad to hear that he's doing so well. Give my regards to your parents."

As she walked away I immediately flashed back to three years ago. Just before the bell had rung, Mrs. Blila had stopped by my table and put her hand on my shoulder. "Kevin, why don't you stay a little after the bell? I have a special project for you."

Any time a teacher tells you to stay after school, you know you're in for it. Tony met my eyes and snickered.

I snickered too.

In first grade, I pretty much copied everything Tony did.

But, when the bell rang, I waited as Mrs. Blila had asked.

When the room was empty, except for the two of us, she turned to me and said, "Kevin, your mom said your father is coming home from the hospital today. We thought it might be nice if you make him a welcome home banner. Would you like that?"

Even then, I knew when adults were saying things they didn't exactly mean. What she meant was, "Kevin, your mom asked me to keep you here a little while after school so she can get your dad settled after she brings him home from the hospital."

But, the idea of making Dad a welcome home banner was pretty appealing so we dug into all the art supplies.

For once, I didn't have to share with anyone.

I could use all the glitter glue I wanted.

I sprinkled on all the confetti that would stick to the places on the poster that had wet glue.

I was in heaven.

Mrs. Blila helped me a little with drawing out the words, "Welcome Home Dad," but after that she just let me do whatever I wanted, only offering a suggestion from time-to time when I wasn't sure what to do next. I'm not sure how long it took, but after a while, she looked at it and said, "Well, Kevin, what do you think?"

I looked down at my masterpiece and knew that my dad would love it.

Things had been a little strained that week.

I wasn't sure what it meant for my dad to be in the hospital, but I knew it wasn't good. The energy in our house was strange.

Hard.

Dark.

A little scary.

Mom didn't smile as often as she used to, and sometimes I would catch her just staring off into space when she didn't think I noticed.

With the poster completed, Mrs. Blila walked me to the front of Webster School and watched as I hopped down the concrete stairs to the sidewalk.

I turned before I crossed the street to my house.

I could still see her standing there, watching me.

I lifted a hand to wave at her before crossing the street and then I jumped into the fragrant pile of yellow elm leaves that filled the big depression in the road right in front of our house.

Wading through the leaves made me feel happy.

Jeanne met me at the front door with a finger to her lips, shushing me even before I had a chance to make any noise, but, she was really nice and helped me to hold up the banner for Dad who was sitting in his gold chair in the living room.

He looked really pale.

And he smelled like stale alcohol from a doctor's office.

But he loved the poster, and, I'll never forget that hug.

He held onto me like he never wanted to let go.

After that, the energy in our house was normal again.

The only difference was that I started hiding his cigars from him. I'd learned in school that smoking wasn't good for you, and Mom helped me by throwing them into the very bottom of the garbage container in the kitchen and then putting wet coffee grounds or something else disgusting on top of them.

Smoking for my dad wasn't a good thing.

Mom had said if I didn't want Dad to go into the hospital again, I should help him to stop smoking.

I sure did try.

Now, as I turned away from Mrs. Blila, I remembered that day as if it had happened yesterday.

I hadn't done such a good job hiding Dad's cigars as I had done before, but I always associated Mrs. Blila with that bright autumn day when Dad's health wasn't as good as the rest of the dads in the neighborhood.

CHAPTER 3

Compared to the rest of the families in our largely second generation immigrant neighborhood, my parents were pretty average.

Dad, John Kevin Kearns, was first-generation Irish Catholic.

Both his parents were "fresh off the boat," settling in Everett, Massachusetts.

Mom, Theresa Cassie, was French-Canadian, but born in Revere, Massachusetts.

My mom and dad, who loved me so well

Mom loved telling us that she married Dad because he was the first guy she could actually tell off. They were only a year apart in age, and yet Mom worried about Dad from the time she met him.

I have to admit I didn't know the whole story behind my dad's health, but the family legend says he wasn't supposed to live much past the age of seventeen; something about him being born with half a liver.

I know, it doesn't make any sense, but I don't know any more to the story than that.

What I can say is that Mom worried about my dad's health for as long as I have memories.

"John, you're eating too much salt."

"John, lay of those cigars, they're not good for you."

"John, you don't have to eat all that meat, think of your cholesterol."

And on it went.

Dad, on the other hand, didn't seem to worry about much. He was an easy-going guy who loved people. Everywhere he went, he knew people by their first name, and they all greeted him by name.

Some of my favorite memories were created during the summers when Dad would take me along for work. He was a building inspector for the city and he took his job seriously.

Most building inspectors strike the fear of God in people.

Not my dad.

Most people loved having my dad come by to inspect their building project.

"Hey Jackie! How's it going today?"

Mom and Dad when they were first married with Dad's mom

"Great, Rudy. What am I looking at? Ah, yeah, I see. Looking good. So, what did you end up doing with those deficiencies I spotted last week?"

"Got 'em handled, just like you asked. Hey, thanks for giving me a little extra time. I wanna do this right."

"I know you do, Rudy."

With that problem handled, we'd head on to the next site and my dad would be greeted with the same kind of respect and friendship at every single job site.

"Hey, Jackie. I'm not quite ready for ya."

"What's going on?"

My dad would move forward, intent on helping rather than hindering.

So many times there would be some kind of deficiency in the work, and my dad always cut them some slack.

He didn't overlook things.

He just pointed things out and then gave them a week or so to fix it before he'd come back. The people whose buildings he inspected knew he would be back and they knew he'd be looking for signs that they had honored their promise.

I remember one time, he went into a building and something wasn't right. He pulled the guy aside and said, "Look, I'm going to let you slide on this, this time, but when I come back next week, you gotta get this done right. If it's not done, I'm gonna have to pull the permit on ya. OK?"

"OK, yeah, thanks, Jackie. I appreciate it. I'm just trying to get it done."

"I understand, but we wanna get it done right, don't we?"

"Yeah, sure, Jackie. I'll have it taken care of by next week."

And it would always be taken care of.

He'd inspect commercial sites.

He'd inspect home additions.

In our neighborhood, everyone was either Irish, Italian or Polish.

One time, we went to a house not far from our immediate neighborhood. Mario, a carpenter, was adding on a porch and Dad was scheduled to inspect it.

"Hey, Mario!" My dad greeted him as we walked around to the backyard to where Mr. Pernelli was working on a porch addition to their house. "Whatchadoin'?"

Mario replied in his broken English, "Putting on a porch," as he talked around his cannoli, wiping his hand on his jeans. There were four kids running around in the garden out back, yelling and hollering in the summer sun.

We had a noisy neighborhood.

Dad looked at what they guy was doing, "Mario, what's going on here? This doesn't go here and that doesn't go there. Come on!" He turned and looked at Mr. Pernelli with a frown on his usually pleasant face, shaking his head.

Mr. Pernelli gave in. "Gimme a break, Jackie. I gotta get it done and I'm just doin' the best I can."

Dad looked out at the kids playing in the yard and we both heard Mrs. Pernelli inside scolding someone in Italian. He shook his head again and I knew he was going to let Mr. Pernelli have a little extra time. "OK, I'll give you a week; you have to figure this out. But ya can't Mickey Mouse this together. You got a family to think about. You want one of your kids to fall offa here?"

They agreed on a time to meet the next week.

And I knew that Mr. Pernelli would have all the problems fixed.

Everyone wanted to please my dad because they wanted their construction projects to keep moving forward. What I admired most was how Dad was able to give people bad news, usually that their building techniques didn't quite meet code, and they never got mad at him. My dad commanded a lot of respect without having to throw his weight around.

Man, I just wanted to grow up to be just like him.

When we left, I climbed back into our '77 Ford Maverick.

Mom said it was tan, but I thought it looked more peach than tan.

It had no power steering and no air conditioning. We'd had another car I had hoped would one day be mine, but my sister had recently totaled it. Now we had a freaking orange car that Dad laughingly said was 55 A/C, meaning we had to go 55-miles-an-hour with the windows rolled down in order to cool off.

I always rolled the windows down because my dad really loved his El Producto cigars.

But I didn't.

He never smoked while I was in the car, but the smell lingered from the times he would smoke in the it when he was alone. It's a smell I always associate with my dad.

Sometimes we'd stop at Brigham's Ice Cream Store for lunch. I always ordered the same thing: a Raspberry Lime Rickey. It's nothing more than soda water, raspberry soda-pop and lime juice, but, at Brighams, they made it with crushed ice, like you had a slushy.

It was delicious.

Everyone like's "Jacky" Kearns

The owner knew Dad by his first name, Jackie. My mother was the only one who called Dad "John." To everyone else, he was "Jackie."

"Hey, Jackie! Coming in for lunch today? And a Raspberry Lime Rickey for Kevin here, right?"

I nodded my head, grinning.

Being greeted by name and having the owner know my favorite drink was heady stuff.

Everyone loved my dad. He knew everyone by first name, and they knew his. Dad was probably the friendliest guy I knew.

The other thing I could never figure out was how much respect people gave my dad.

He had power, certainly, but never exerted it. He was able to go up to somebody, and, in an instant, there was a friendly rapport between them.

I watched it happen over and over, time and again, and I would run it through my mind, trying to figure out how he did it.

I could never figure out how he did it.

I wanted to be just like my dad.

But at that time, I could only watch him and wish I had what he had.

※　※　※　※　※

One summer evening, Tony and I were out later than usual.

We had managed to trick our respective moms into giving us permission to stay outside even after the streetlights had come on.

We sat in Webster schoolyard, just outside the circle of glowing light from the streetlamp, our backs against the chain-link fence, listening to the hypnotic sound of the chirping crickets. Being a warm night, they chirped at a very rapid rate, and the sound seemed so loud in the absence of anything else.

We'd reach up from time to time and pick one of "Mr. Italy's" raspberries and I puckered my mouth when I got one that wasn't quite as ripe as it could have been.

This made the ripe ones taste so much sweeter.

Some moments just feel perfect, and, for just that moment, my life felt pretty good. A soft night breeze helped us to cool off from the heat radiating through our sneaker-shod feet from the blacktop of the schoolyard.

Beside me Tony fidgeted, first with his fingers, then it migrated down to his feet that began tapping in a staccato rhythm, drowning out the soothing sound of the crickets.

I let out a big sigh.

I knew what was coming.

He jumped to his feet and said, "Come on, let's do something before we have to go in!"

Tony always had to be the center of attention, and, sitting in the dark shadows of the schoolyard wasn't feeding his need. He got up, started running toward Jefferson Avenue, shouting at me over his shoulder, "Come on, Kevin!"

I obeyed, quickly catching up to him.

With darkness covering our neighborhood I felt pretty invisible.

Lights glowed inside everyone's home and even if they looked out their windows, they couldn't tell who we were.

During the daytime, I would never agree to getting into mischief.

It was too hard to get away with it.

The neighbors would tell Mom or Dad and then I'd be in for it then.

The neighborhood was the neighborhood.

Everyone watched out for everybody else, and they knew everyone's business.

Under the cover of darkness, things were different.

At first, I feared that Tony would leave the well known streets of our neighborhood, but it seemed like he was just blowing off steam, turning around, running back through the schoolyard and back to Dartmouth Street.

Just then, the lights of a car heading down Jefferson Avenue caught Tony's attention.

"Hey Kevin, watch this!"

Tony picked up a wad of paper and just chucked it at the car heading down the street, but it didn't have enough weight to travel much more than a few feet. With a grunt of disgust, Tony pounced on a rock about the size of a pack of chewing gum.

He did a perfect baseball windup and then just let it go.

We just stood there, frozen in that moment in time.

I kept thinking, "Nah, there's no way he's going to hit it…no way…I hope."

It landed with a loud crack on the windshield.

"Oh shit!" Tony shouted. "Run!"

We both bolted.

The car followed us.

Hearing my heart beat in my ears, I followed Tony through a couple of back yards, hopping over darkened lumps that were tricycles or garden stools. It made sense at the time, but we'd forgotten that Jefferson was a one-way street, so when we doubled back we figured we weren't going to get caught.

I mindlessly followed Tony.

He was the leader of this mission, not me. So when we burst through the bushes right alongside the street, I expected the street to be empty.

The driver exploded from his car.

I looked with horror at him.

He was missing his right arm.

My stomach clenched.

How had Tony's rock managed to cut off this guy's arm?

"What are you kids thinking?" He sounded pretty mad, his voice strong and vigorous. Too vigorous to have suffered such a serious injury.

Tony didn't seem to have any qualms about what he had done.

"Sorry, Mister! This kid we were hanging out with, Mike, he's from New Hampshire. He threw that rock."

"We told him not to, but he threw it anyway."

Tony started telling the lie and I added details just out of nowhere.

I knew it was wrong.

We'd cracked the windshield of a one-armed man and I was lying to get out of it.

The guy hollered at us for a few minutes, but eventually he got in his car and drove away, down Jefferson Street.

I looked at Tony and muttered, "I gotta go in now."

I ran home, up the stairs into the house and made no fuss about going to bed. I huddled there in the darkness thinking about how black my soul must look.

I don't know why I'd just gone along with Tony.

When the rock he'd thrown cracked against the windshield of the one-armed man's car, I felt as though I had crossed a line and I didn't like how it felt.

※　※　※　※　※

The next Saturday afternoon, I was working on one of my airplane models. Dad came over to where I worked, carefully cutting apart the pieces of my F4U4 Corsair Fighter model airplane.

He placed his cup of coffee down on the table and pulled up a chair.

"What can I do to help?" he asked.

I passed over the fuselage where the retractable landing gear had to be attached. I'd managed to put together a few model airplane kits that were pretty straightforward, but this kit had gear bay doors that opened and closed, folding wings, armament drop tanks, bombs, and rockets, and a rotating prop.

I could use his help.

As Dad had taught me, I removed all the parts from the box and spread them out, checking each one against the instruction sheet to make sure I had all the parts I needed.

While Dad read the instructions for the retractable gear, I got two toothpicks from the kitchen to hold the wheels while I painted them. They had to be painted and dried before they could be put on the airplane.

We worked in silence for a while, passing the x-acto knife back and forth, with the sharp point away from us, as we needed to remove the plastic spurs that stuck on some of the airplane parts. Each joint had to be perfectly smooth before any glue was applied. Dad had taught me to use just enough glue to keep the parts together. Some of my first models had excess blobs of glue that spoiled the model's appearance. In other places, the glue had actually melted the join area because I'd used too much.

Today, I deftly applied the thinnest lines of glue before holding the model pieces together.

Dad watched me as he sipped his coffee, nodding in approval.

Once everything was glued together, it was time to wait for it to be completely cemented before moving on. Another lesson I'd had to learn the hard way.

As we both sat admiring our handiwork, Dad cleared his throat.

Uh-oh.

I knew what was coming.

"You were out pretty late last night."

Just an observation, but coming from my dad, it was more than just an observation.

"Yeah."

My brain raced to see how I could spin the story.

"I heard about some boys chucking rocks at cars."

Again, he was just making a statement only.

No accusation.

But as he took a sip of his coffee his eyes met mine and I couldn't break the stare.

Trapped.

I said nothing.

Dad's right eyebrow arched as he tilted his head to the side. "You know anything about that?"

My mind raced for the right thing to say. Finally I blurted out, "Tony threw the rock.

As Dad nodded his head thoughtfully, I realized I needed to come clean.

"I was with him, but I didn't throw anything. Honest!"

"You know, don't you, that you have to be careful who you hang out with?"

My head nodded furiously. "Yeah, I do."

"Tony sometimes lets his impulses get the better of him. I think you're more careful than that. Next time, come inside on time. Nothing good ever happens at night."

Again, I nodded, my eyes still caught by his penetrating stare.

"OK, then. I'm thinking of going to Chelsea Theater to see Charlton Heston in Midway. You interested in coming?"

Really?

I wasn't going to die today?

"Sure!"

"Get ready then, we need to leave in ten minutes."

And with that, Dad ended one of my most uncomfortable conversations with him. I'd told the truth, and that's what mattered to him. He'd believed me when I said I hadn't thrown any rocks. As tempted as I had been to lie about being with Tony, I was so relieved that I'd made the right choice.

That afternoon with my Dad was even better than our usual Saturday afternoons watching *Creature Double Feature* where we would argue over the various attributes of Godzilla versus King Kong.

Sitting next to Dad in the theater, munching on buttered popcorn and drinking a soda, I figured I was the luckiest kid in the world.

I had the greatest Dad ever.

CHAPTER 4

"When's Dad coming home?"

Mom kept her back turned to me, and, at first I thought she hadn't heard me. Then, as she scrubbed a spot on the counter with unnecessary vigor, she responded, "Soon, Kevin. Soon."

I waited for her to say more, but she kept on working, wiping the counters, even picking up the toaster to wipe away the crumbs underneath. She seemed to be intent on attacking every bit of food or dust, visible or invisible.

Taking advantage of her inattention, I spooned more sugar into my cereal bowl. The metal top clanked against the ceramic base with a little tink.

Usually this made her protest that I was using too much sugar.

I waited, holding my breath. But this time it was as if she hadn't heard. As I chewed, I watched her, looking at her back. She moved mechanically, sometimes really fast, sometimes as if her inner switch had been set to half speed.

Ever since Dad had gone to the hospital, the very energy in our house changed. Mom's ready smile had disappeared. The worry lines between her eyebrows deepened, never smoothing out.

"You're sad Dad won't be able to go out and get you a Valentine's Day gift, aren't you?"

I put another spoonful of cereal in my mouth, chewed and swallowed it before she responded, "Yeah Kevin. That's it."

I'd last been to see my dad in the hospital just the previous weekend. He had been incredibly drawn and his skin was pale. When we talked, he was obviously making great effort to pay attention to what I was saying, and anytime we stopped talking for a bit, he put his head back on the pillows and seemed to take a little catnap.

But everytime I started talking again, he raised his head, looked at me intently and just listened.

That's one of the things I loved the most about my dad, the way he listened to whatever I had to say as if it were really important.

I remember I had been telling him about Patty in my 7th grade class at school.

I was twelve and this was probably my first real crush on a girl.

His eyes had twinkled as I talked and he had a little smile on his face.

I could tell he was proud I was interested in a girl.

I rinsed my bowl and left it in the sink.

Mom was in another one of her half-speed phases, wiping the top of the stove over and over. I left her to her thoughts.

I, too, had a Valentine responsibility.

From the first time our eyes met, Patty at school had turned me from a guy who felt all girls had cooties to a struggling mess of emotions inside. The minute she had smiled at me in homeroom class, I was snared.

Her Valentine had to be perfect in every way, and I'd saved most of my newspaper money to get it. I'd slipped it into her desk on Friday afternoon, but hadn't seen her find it.

My gut was churning to know what she thought of it.

The next morning I woke up early, even before my alarm went off. I lazed in bed for a few minutes, soaking up all the cozy warmth before getting up for my morning paper route.

Not wanting to wake my mom or sister, I silently put on my winter coat and hat. I couldn't find my gloves, and, at first, I was tempted to do without them, but the thought of the frozen handlebars on my yellow-orange Huffy bike made me look harder.

No gloves.

In disgust, I opened my drawer where I knew I had a pair of mittens; clumsy and awkward, but they would at least keep my fingers from freezing. Still tiptoeing, I let myself out of the house with just the barest of clicks of the door, still sharply audible in the crisp darkness of the winter morning. My breath fogged before me, reflected by the street lamps.

Most houses up and down Dartmouth street were dark, their inhabitants still asleep.

Not me.

I had a job to do.

It was only six months ago that I had landed this paper route job.

Dad was so proud of me.

I'd managed to secure the job all on my own.

My bike that led to my first job: delivering newspapers.

At first, it was really hard getting up before the rest of the world. But after a few weeks, I liked being awake while everyone else slept.

I felt like I knew a secret no one else knew.

My bike squeaked and clanked in the frigid air as I pedaled up to the end of Madison Avenue where it intersected with Elm Street. As I approached, I could see the dark shape of the stack of newspapers waiting for me.

As I had suspected, it was impossible to fold and rubber-band them with my mittens on so I pulled them off and stuffed them into my jacket pockets.

You learn to work fast in winter.

This was the coldest part of the job because I wasn't moving to keep warm and the cold-soaked papers were stiff and resisted my frozen fingers.

Once or twice, I put the mittens back on and then, cupping my hands in front of my mouth, blew warm air into them to bring some circulation back to my fingertips.

The instant the last paper was folded, I hopped on my bike and flew off. The first couple weeks I had my route, I had to stop at each house, check the address and then aim for the door or porch, wherever each house wanted their paper delivered.

Now, I was faster.

My route memorized, I didn't have to stop and aim anymore.

I could toss the papers on the fly.

In the winter, this was especially important. I prided myself on the fact that only once did I have to ask Dad for help because the snow was so deep I couldn't plow through it with my bike, and it was impossible to walk through.

He drove me that morning, and I could still hear how he laughed as I shared stories about each of my customers. Everytime I got back inside the warm car, I felt protected and cherished.

That had been a special morning.

This morning, the wind whipped at my face, and there was no warm car to jump into.

I hoped Dad would be home soon.

It wasn't that I wanted him to drive me for my paper route, I just really didn't like for him to be gone so long at the hospital.

Since today was a holiday, I could go and visit him again.

With that thought in mind, I raced against the coming dawn. I always tried to be home before it was light. It made me feel secretive and accomplished to have delivered everyone's paper before they had even had their first cup of coffee.

As I approached the house, I frowned.

There was a dark car on Clarence Street.

Right beside our house.

I didn't remember seeing it there when I left.

Now I noticed the lights from inside the house glowing on the snow just outside in the yard. Through the kitchen window, I could see a silhouette of my mom.

It looked like she was holding herself up on the counter with her elbows.

Unusual.

Because it was a holiday, she would normally still be sleeping.

There was no point in stealth.

It looked like something was up.

I bounded up the steps to the front door and shivered a bit as the warmth of the house surrounded me. I could hear a murmur of voices from the kitchen as I tossed my mittens, hat, and coat down.

Just as I reached the doorway to the kitchen, my dad's best friend, Ray, came out.

"Kevin, we were wondering when you'd be back."

Now this was weird.

Why was Dad's friend here?

My heart leaped, maybe Dad was home!

"Is Dad here?" I didn't even try to keep the excitement out of my voice.

Ray's face folded into an expression I couldn't read.

It almost looked like he was tasting something bitter.

"Come here, Kevie."

Even though I was twelve, he picked me up like I was a little kid and set me on the wooden box where I kept my toys.

"Ray, what's wrong? Why are you here?"

"Kevie, I have some really bad news for you."

He swallowed hard.

And again.

"Your Dad died early this morning."

I stared at Ray.

The words weren't processing.

He was kidding.

He had to be kidding.

Without warning, I started laughing hysterically. "You're kidding, Ray, right? That's a lousy joke, but I know you're kidding!"

My voice got higher and higher.

Mom moved to where I could see her in the doorway of the kitchen. She was crying, her face wet with tears.

"Mom?" My voice sounded strangled.

All she could do was nod her head, small, sharp nods, her face crumpling as she did so and more tears erupted from her eyes.

"No!" I screamed. "He can't be dead!"

I gasped for breath, I felt as though I'd been punched in the stomach.

How?

Why?

And then I collapsed into grief and guilt.

I hadn't made Dad his Valentine's Day card because I was so worked up about Patty's card.

It was my fault!

It had to be!

If only I had made his card sooner.

I felt Ray's hard arms pick me up and he held me as if I were still a little boy. I choked, and screamed, and got tears and snot and saliva all over my dad's best friend's shirt. I don't know how long I cried, it seemed like forever. At one point, I was gasping for breath, feeling like I was blacking out, and all the while Ray's strong arms just held me, holding me close, sometimes moving from side to side as if he were rocking a baby.

Visions ran through my mind.

Dad and me building models.

One of the models I built with Dad

Watching *Creature Double Feature*.

Eating raspberry-lime Rickey's at Brigham's Ice Cream Store.

Just a few minutes ago, I was remembering that wonderful morning early in December when he had driven me on my route because it had snowed so much.

That had been such a great morning.

Now Ray was telling me there were going to be no more mornings like that one.

Ever.

His voice in my ear shushed me. It told me it was OK to cry, and told me everything was going to be OK.

But it wasn't.

Nothing would ever be OK again.

How could Dad be dead?

I'd just seen him the other day at the hospital. OK, so he hadn't looked so great with all those tubes and things coming out of him, but he hadn't looked like he would die.

Hiccupping and softly sobbing, I lifted my head from Ray's shoulder and looked again at my mom, framed in the doorway of the kitchen.

"When did he die? Were you there?"

Mom had a hard time answering. It took her three tries before she could control her voice. "The hospital called while you were asleep. They thought I should be there."

Just then Jeanne came up behind my mom. She was awake and in the kitchen too. In fact, I realized that they were still wearing the clothes they had worn yesterday.

"Jeanne was there too? She got to say goodbye to Dad too? Why didn't you take me?" I screamed at her. "I wanted to see him again too!"

Ray's arms still held me tight and his voice started talking to me in my ear . . . soft and slow, rough with his own grief. "They weren't sure, Kevie, that he was dying. Your mom didn't want to wake you in case it was a false alarm. By the time we knew, it was too late. We hurried home, but you had already left to do your paper route."

I struggled to process what Ray was saying.

No one had been home when I got up?

Sure the house had been quiet, but I hadn't realized it was empty.

"Come on, Buddy, you're going to have to be the man of the house now."

What the hell did he mean by that?

I was twelve for God's sake!

My stomach was churning and I struggled out of Ray's arms and ran to the bathroom where I retched and vomited even though there was nothing in my stomach. This time it was my mom's cool hands rubbing my back, wringing out a wet washcloth to wipe my face and the back of my neck.

"Kevin, I'm sorry. I'm so, so sorry."

Her words whispered over and over.

She was trying to make it better.

My heart was broken and I had no room for forgiveness.

She hadn't told me.

She hadn't gotten me up so I could see Dad one last time.

I jerked away from her and went into my room in the foyer. Ignoring the fact that my boots were still wet from the snow, I flung myself on my bed where I started crying again, this time soft and anguished.

I cried until I was empty and there were no more tears.

Perhaps I slept for a little while, but when I opened my eyes, it was still pretty early in the day.

More voices were coming from the kitchen.

I listened carefully.

Aunt Dee and Uncle Henry.

Of course they would be the first to arrive, they lived just a few blocks away.

I rolled over onto my back and stared up at the ceiling, my eyes swollen and scratchy. Every now and then, a tear would roll out of my eye and into my ear.

So this was grief.

Loss.

I wasn't sure what I was supposed to feel like. I'd just responded to Ray's words.

There was no thought.

I really thought at first he was kidding. Ray was such a kidder, but once I realized he was being serious, I felt as though I had lost my mind. My nose was so swollen I couldn't breathe out of it, so I had to breathe through my mouth.

Suddenly I was trying to breathe in great big gasps of air, but it was as if my body had forgotten how to breathe.

My diaphragm was in spasm, moving opposite the way it was supposed to.

I became dizzy and my vision blacked out.

In a frantic attempt to breathe, I pushed myself to a half-sitting position, struggling to breathe, strange whistling sounds coming from my throat.

Was I going to die too?

Just as I was ready to go into full-fledged panic mode, a soft hand stroked the side of my face, and I felt a weight on the side of my bed. Another hand reached around and helped me sit all the way up.

Aunt Dee.

"Just breathe, Kevin. Slow down there. You just need to catch your breath." Her words seemed to hypnotize me, and I found myself calming down.

She just kept repeating, over and over, "I'm here, Kevin. I love you. I'll be here for you."

Pretty soon, the panic receded and I was able to reach up around her neck and then held on for dear life. I started crying again. Not the loud, hysterical sobs that erupted when Ray had first told me. These were the deepest outpouring of grief, straight from inside me, from the very depths of my heart.

I cried for my dad.

I cried because we would never have our special times together again.

I cried because I didn't know what else to do.

My emotions battled with one another: sadness, anger, fear, and a vicious feeling deep inside that made me afraid of what I might do.

The more I tried to ignore it, the more afraid of it I became.

What was this thing inside of me, this vicious being who wanted to rip apart everyone near me? It had appeared to me a few times before, when Tony and Paul had pestered me, but I knew I had to subdue it, and I had always been in control.

Today, as Aunt Dee held me, I didn't think it would be so easy to control anymore. It seemed as though grief fed this monster inside of me.

It was growing faster than I could contain it.

The next hours passed in a blur.

I spent it either in my bedroom or sitting in Dad's chair in the living room. As the day wore on and more and more people heard about Dad's death, our house got busier, louder. People came in and embraced Mom. I couldn't help but watch her suspiciously.

Her tears were certainly real enough.

Did she really not know Dad was going to die?

How could she not wake me?

Why?

Each question evoked feelings inside that fed the frightening beast inside of me. Every time I noticed myself getting angry, I had to calm down. This anger was white-hot, fierce, and more powerful than I was.

I was afraid of what I might do if I just let it go.

People came and went.

Over and over, the front door opened, each time bringing with it a fresh gust of frigid air.

They brought tears and hugs and words of comfort.

They brought cakes and casseroles.

On any other day, I would have been the happiest kid on the block to know I could have cake everyday for the next three weeks. Now, I just watched the food start to pile up in the kitchen.

I felt no hunger.

My stomach had clenched into a hard, little ball, as if it never wanted to eat again.

Aunt Dee came out of the kitchen and sat down next to me. I was staring at the television, even though it wasn't turned on. She just sat there for a minute, not saying anything. I was glad she didn't put her arm around me right then. I wasn't feeling the heat of anger right now, but I was so weak and tired and I knew it wouldn't take a whole lot to get me crying again, and, I was pretty much done crying.

What had Ray said? *You're the man of the house now.*

Well, the man of the house couldn't be a cry baby.

After sitting together for a couple of minutes, Aunt Dee said, "I think I want to get out of here for a bit. Would you like to come with me?"

I thought about it for a few seconds and then nodded.

Except for Aunt Dee and Uncle Henry, I felt invisible.

As people came in, carrying their cakes and casseroles, they glanced at me sitting in Dad's chair and then looked away and made their way into the kitchen. The rise in the pitch of voices in the kitchen told me Mom noticed them there. When it got really quiet again, I knew they were hugging and crying. Soon, they would start talking again and the murmur of voices reached a new sort of normal level.

No one wanted to come out and talk to me.

The house felt empty and cold, even though we had more people in it now than we ever had during a party. Because Dad wasn't here, there was a huge, gaping void in the fabric of our home life.

Somehow I had to get used to it.

He was never coming back.

I finally looked up and nodded at my Aunt Dee, who was waiting patiently for me to get up. Her gentle hand on my shoulder gave me a quick squeeze. "Go get your coat and we'll get out of here."

She understood.

Her eyes were bright with unshed tears and her mouth, usually smiling and colored with lipstick was pale and being held in a firm line, only faltering for a second before she regained control and gave me a quick smile.

The day was surprisingly sunny.

I knew it was unreasonable to be angry about something as natural as sunshine. Because of what had happened, I thought the skies should at least cooperate and be filled with the usual steel-gray clouds that proclaimed winter in Massachusetts. I scowled at the sky while I waited for my aunt to get into the driver's seat of the car.

Aunt Dee started the car and we pulled away from the curb. My chest felt so tight, I thought for a moment I was suffocating, and against my will, a huge sob erupted and I found myself crying in the front seat next to my Aunt Dee who was sniffing quietly herself. She reached over and squeezed my shoulder sympathetically as she just stared out the windshield while we rode along in silence, except for when we sniffed and snuffled together.

Finally, I felt some connection to someone.

At home, I was stared at and I could hear the whispers about "poor little Kevin" but no one came over to me or hugged me. Aunt Dee wasn't afraid to be with me, to talk with me, to cry with me. I'd been feeling really isolated and alone, which helped me to just keep most of my emotions bottled up inside of me. The ride to the department store to get me clothes for Dad's funeral with Aunt Dee gave us a sense of solidarity with one another.

We shopped, mostly in silence, for a set of dark clothes to wear to Dad's funeral. Shopping had never been an activity I looked forward to. I usually just grabbed the first things that looked like they'd work, just like I did when my mom took me shopping for school clothes.

Aunt Dee frowned slightly at my choices and said, "I think we need to pick out something that suits you better."

For the first time in my life, I found myself following her through the department store as she picked out a shirt, pants, and then a tie and a jacket.

To mark my father's death, I would wear a tie and a jacket.

Ray's words continued haunting my thoughts. *Kevie, now you're the man of the house.*

I was only twelve.

How could I be the man of the house?

I was only just figuring out how to be the kid of the house.

I started thinking about our "three-family" on Dartmouth Street. Our house was well built, but as far as homes go, it was big and boxy, and really, really yellow. Dad had planned to paint it a different color, but I had no clue as the new "man of the house" how to change the color of our house. Good, old Mrs. Davis on the second floor was probably with my mother right now helping her through what was likely the worst day of her life. Our third floor tenants came and went on a regular basis. All they would notice is that there were a lot of cars parked around our house and the block than usual. I couldn't even remember who was renting the third floor of our home right now.

Time started and stopped that day.

Before I knew it, we were pulling up in front of our house on Dartmouth street, stopping and taking the bags of purchases from the trunk. I couldn't remember when I'd gotten so many new clothes at one time. The late day sun cast long shadows on the front of the house, and, if I imagined hard enough, I could remember the last time I climbed those stairs and heard my Dad's voice the instant I entered the house.

Today, it was missing.

All I heard when we entered the house was the same murmur of voices that had been there when Aunt Dee and I left.

I wanted to turn around and run down the block, and keep on running until whatever terrified me had been left far behind.

Aunt Dee looked at me.

Again, I had the incredible sense that she understood exactly what I was thinking and she guided me through the same door I had opened when I finished my paper route that morning.

Only this time, I knew my Dad was never going to be inside again.

My cousin Kenny was there, hovering just outside the kitchen when we came in the front door. The instant he spied me, he came over, got down on his knees, and just hugged me. He was quite a bit older than I was, but I loved him for the fact he didn't try to do anything but recognize how much I was hurting inside.

He took me into the living room where the television was on, but the volume was muted.

Together we sat together in my dad's old chair and just stared at the images that flickered on the television screen.

It didn't matter what was showing right then.

What mattered was Kenny's arms around me as if they wouldn't let go.

CHAPTER 5

THE WAKE

We were at the funeral home, and, once again, surrounded by people who wanted to talk about Dad. We'd gathered for another rosary service because so many people had wanted to attend that the funeral home had to schedule three services.

Father Walsh led us in saying the rosary.

I responded in a barely audible monotone.

The smell of the flowers made me miserable.

I looked around.

No one looked happy to be here. So why did they want to come? I refused to look at the casket, at Dad. Everyone around me kept saying, "He looks so good. Doesn't he look good?"

How could he look good?

He's dead!

The smell of the flowers must have been affecting everyone. I kept telling myself that my runny nose was due to the fragrance of all the flowers that surrounded the casket. There were pots of white lilies, and wreaths of red and yellow roses. There were huge arrangements of flowers that looked almost like fireworks, they were so big and spiky.

If Dad had been there, he would have snickered at them.

That made me smile . . . a little.

Now there wasn't a thing he could do about it. He was trapped in a long wooden box with those ridiculous things all around him, rising in a small mountain at his feet.

I hadn't meant to look at him, but once my glance fell upon my dad's face, I couldn't turn away. I started gulping really big gulps, swallowing air and tears. I wasn't going to cry again, not in front of all these people. There were a few of my friends from school there with their parents, and they stood in line to talk to my mother, but I refused to stand up there with her.

My refusal had nothing to do with being disrespectful of my mom or my dad. It had everything to do with not knowing what I was going to do.

As each hour wore on, I felt feelings I couldn't name.

They were big and dark, hot and wet.

What if they grew so much that I choked on them?

What if I suddenly went absolutely berserk and started running wild in the room, tearing the flowers from their stems, raining red and yellow and orange petals all around the room like confetti?

What if I gave in to my deepest impulse to reach into the casket and grab my dad by his suit-covered shoulders and shake him until he gasped for breath and lived again?

Just to hear him breathe one more time, to hug his warm and living body, and say, "I love you."

"Hail Mary, full of grace," the words rose and fell in a huge wave of murmurings in the overheated, heavily perfumed room. The cloying sweetness of the flowers mingled with fragrance, aftershave, sweat, candle wax, and tears resulted in a noxious aroma cloud that enveloped everyone in the room.

"Holy Mary, Mother of God," someone burst into tears as if begging the Mother of God to bring her peace.

I peeked up.

It was my mother.

Her shoulders shook as Aunt Dee held her around her waist, a damp wad of tissues clamped under her nose.

Father Walsh grimly marched on through the litany of prayers, clearing his thickened voice occasionally.

My knees ached.

My fingers were locked against the backs of my hands as I held them together as I'd been taught in Sunday school, the pain a welcome distraction from what was going on in the room.

Not one single kid in my class came to talk to me when the rosary was done and the prayer vigil concluded. They'd hung close to their parents, barely even glancing up, certainly not looking at the casket. I envied them their set of healthy-appearing parents, but knew that I would reject even the smallest sign of pity in their eyes.

I backed into a far corner of the room.

Determined to be as small and invisible as possible.

From my vantage point at the back of the room, I could squint my swollen eyes against the bright flames of the candles, and, it almost seemed as if Dad was only sleeping. For the briefest moment, my heart leaped when I thought I saw his chest rise and fall as if he'd taken a breath, but, when I opened my eyes wide and stared at his chest until they were scratchy and dry, there wasn't a single movement. The funeral director stepped in front of the casket blocking my view. When he moved away, the candles had been extinguished and Dad's face was in the shadows.

He looked as dead as ever.

* * * * *

Jeanne and me; the picture was a Christmas gift for my parents right before dad died

THE FUNERAL

Ever since Dad died, Mom, Jeanne, and I slept in Mom and Dad's bedroom.

Jeanne slept in bed with Mom.

I slept at the foot of the bed on a cot.

None of us wanted to sleep alone.

But we were.

Alone.

During the night, I would wake to soft sobs coming from the bed. At first, I couldn't tell whether it was Mom or Jeanne crying, but it didn't take me long to distinguish each one's unique sounds of grief.

I tried not to cry.

When I was awake, I could fight the feeling when I felt its unwelcome arrival. It wasn't quite so easy when I slept; my dreams took over my will, and I would waken to Mom's gentle touch as she stroked my back until I quieted and fell back asleep.

The morning of Dad's funeral dawned with an irreverent, bright sun. For the second time, I knew it was illogical to be angry with the sun for shining, but it seemed to me as if the world should be darkened out of respect for our loss.

Again, Aunt Dee and Uncle Henry arrived at the house to take Mom, Jeanne, and me to St. Therese's for the funeral. As we pulled up to the nearly fifty-year old church, my memories flashed back to my First Communion celebration.

Mom and Dad had been so proud of me.

It was the first time I remembered wearing a tie and dark dress pants with shoes polished so well I could almost see my face in them.

Dad had taken out his shoe-polishing kit the night before and said, "Kevin, you're going to learn how to polish your shoes."

"John, don't let him get his hands dirty," called Mom from the kitchen.

Dad winked and nodded reassuringly at me. "Get me some newspaper, son."

I hustled over to the pile of newspapers, bringing back more than enough to cover the ugly carpet where we would be working. We both sat cross-legged with the newspaper between us. Dad had brought out his black shoes and said, "I'll show you how to do it, and then you'll shine yours. How's that sound?"

Sounded great to me!

I loved anything my dad wanted to teach me.

I watched carefully as he picked up a wooden handled tool with bristles that seemed stuck together. As he pressed the bristles into the tin of polish, I could see that unlike dried paint, the bristles were still flexible and just covered with black polish.

He rubbed polish all over the outside of first one shoe and then the next one. Then, he carefully turned the tool around so I could take it by the clean handle end. "Go ahead and get some polish on that brush there." I swirled it inside the tin just as I had seen him do and then picked up my smaller shoe and smeared polish against the black leather.

"Make sure you get it in all the crevices."

I rubbed polish on to the shoe and when I went back for more, Dad cautioned, "You don't need a whole lot more, just use what you have on the brush right now. You can get more polish for your other shoe." So I went on rubbing and rubbing until Dad was satisfied I'd gotten the shoe all covered and then moved on to the next one. Once I was done, he wiped the bristles as clean as possible with a piece of newspaper and carefully put it in the trash.

"Don't want to get polish on your Mom's nice carpet here," he said as he winked at me.

"Now, let's take this big buffing brush and make these shoes shine." He showed me how he buffed his shoe, breathing warm breath onto parts that weren't polishing to his satisfaction before moving to the next section.

"This part takes the longest, but it's where you show people you really know what you're doing. When you leave parts of your shoe unshined, you tell the world you don't care how you do things."

"I know, Dad."

I'd heard him say this over and over again.

Things just weren't worth doing unless you did them exactly right.

He handed the buffing brush to me I buffed and huffed just as he'd done. When my hands got tired, he'd take over and help me out until they were rested again. He always let me do the final buffing, which made me feel like I was doing the job exactly right.

Today, as we waited for traffic to clear to park in the parking lot, I stared down at my shoes. I hadn't thought to polish them for the funeral. Tears stung my eyes as I imagined how disappointed Dad might be at me for showing up at his funeral without my shoes polished.

Uncle Henry opened the back door for Mom, and held her hand as she got out of the car.

He did the same for Jeanne.

When it was my turn, I ignored his hand as I scrambled out of the car, but I didn't pull away when he clapped his hand on my shoulder and gave it a squeeze.

Together we climbed the cement flight of stairs up to the great wooden doors that opened into the very long church where we had attended Mass every Sunday since I could remember. Mom grabbed the metal railing, pulling herself up each step just like the older scarf-covered immigrant women from the neighborhood did. For a moment, I was knocked out of my own dark pool of self-pity as I watched her painful progress up the steps. Suddenly, she no longer seemed like the light-hearted, fun-loving girl who danced to Lawrence Welk on Saturday nights in our living room.

She looked old, tired.

Her face had great lines around her mouth as if she were using great effort to hold her lips in place.

Jeanne, too, looked older, wiser.

At eighteen, she was just an adult and she'd lost her dad too.

Again, Ray's words echoed in my mind. *You'll have to be the man of the house now, Kevie.*

I moved ahead of Aunt Dee and Uncle Henry, who had both put their hands on my shoulders. It wasn't that I was rejecting their love and support. It was time I showed my mom and my sister some love and support. I hustled up between the two and reached for their hands. Mom gave me a wordless look, her lips moved fractionally into a grateful smile and the three of us entered the church where Father Walsh would preside over the funeral of the man who had meant the world to the three of us.

At the very least, we would shoulder this burden together. More flowers, more candles. Incense being lit at the back of the church could be smelled deep inside the church, but, fortunately, the soaring ceiling would collect the majority of the smells and keep me from gagging.

The organ signaled the solemn procession with the priest and altar servers walking up the central aisle, the start of the funeral. For the first time in my life, I sat in the front row at church between Mom and Jeanne.

Family and friends filled the pews behind us.

I didn't look around until the final prayers and blessing had been given.

I'd kept my gaze averted even during Communion. When I did look around, I was absolutely shocked. The church was so full ,it was standing room only. I'd known my dad had been a very special man and knew a lot of people, but this outpouring of support and sympathy stunned me.

※　※　※　※　※

THE BURIAL

As we processed out of St. Therese, I glanced across the street, and there on the corner of Broadway and Edith, was the little corner store where Dad would go to buy his El Producto cigars. I remembered plenty of Sundays when he'd nod toward the little store as if asking my mother for permission to go and get some cigars.

She always shook her head and he'd smile like a little kid.

I know he went later because he always had cigars to smoke.

Even though the cemetery was almost directly behind St. Therese, the procession to the burial site had to go down Broadway, the longest street in Everett, before traveling around to the entrance of the cemetery.

Looking through the back window, the line of cars seemed to go on forever.

I knew they were all heading to the burial because they all had their lights on and each car kept a small space between them and the car ahead of them.

It looked like a long, shiny caterpillar.

At the cemetery, the grave site was ready with Dad's casket in place over it.

By now I was numb.

I didn't hear the words Father Walsh said. I just remember having a rose in my hand and following my mother's example of putting it on top of the casket just before it was lowered into the ground.

I wanted to turn away, and run home as fast as my legs could carry me.

Instead, I was stuck here, watching as the last of the casket disappeared beneath the level of the ground. Mom tried to turn me away before they began filling in the grave, but I stubbornly held my position, listening to the sound of dirt covering the shiny top of the casket, the roses we had placed on top, and the last remaining bits of my life with Dad in it.

My chest and throat ached with unshed tears.

My eyes burned from my effort to keep them wide open, thinking if I did so, I wouldn't cry again.

"Bye, Dad," I whispered.

Only then did I yield to my mom's pressure on my shoulder, allowing myself to be turned away and guided back to the car. Only one more performance...the reception back at the house, and it would all be over.

Once in the car, Mom turned around and softly asked, "Kevin, you OK?"

I nodded woodenly, but I couldn't look at her.

I could hear the tightness in her own throat and knew if I looked at her, I would simply explode from my grief. She gazed at me for another moment or two and then turned back around to face the front of the car. Sitting beside me, Jeanne reached for my hand and we sat together in the back seat, holding hands, staring straight ahead saying nothing.

We were all grieving together.

Yet separately.

As if we lived on different continents.

※　※　※　※　※

THE RECEPTION

Back at the house, people arrived before we did. Cars parked clear up and down both Dartmouth and Elsie Streets.

I'd never seen so many cars in our neighborhood before.

Inside was a crowd of people, talking, laughing, eating.

It was like a party.

And I had nowhere to hide.

My bedroom was really part of the foyer, there was no privacy there. I pulled my tie off and threw it on my bed and my jacket followed. It didn't make sense to keep wearing what I called a "monkey suit" now that everything was over. At the kitchen door, I peeked in and saw Mom and Jeanne pulling serving spoons out of the drawers and looking for extra napkins. Their movements were swift and focused, almost as if they would just melt into the floor with sadness if they weren't doing this job.

For the first time, I wondered what they were feeling.

How were we going to live?

Even when Dad was alive, we never had a lot.

As a kid, whenever I lost a tooth, I got a quarter while Tony crowed about the dollar he got.

Mom was relatively young.

Her hair was still dark brown and when she smiled, she looked really pretty.

Today, her face was like a mask.

She smiled and laughed when someone said something to lighten the mood, but then her face would slip back into its mask-like position.

This wasn't any easier on her than it was on me.

How was I going to be the man of the house and take care of her?

I wasn't even a teenager yet.

Dad hadn't lived long enough to see me turn thirteen.

A hand on my shoulder made me turn and look up. Aunt Dee smiled a sad, sweet smile at me. "You need anything to eat, Kevin?" At least she was smart enough not to ask me how I was feeling.

I shook my head.

"What are you thinking about?"

It took me a few moments to figure out how to answer her question. "I'm thinking that anger is better than sadness. I'm done with being sad." With those words, I could feel a strange sense of power come over me but rather than making me feel good, it frightened me.

"Oh, you'll come around, Kevin. But it's going to take time."

I shook my head with hard sharp movements. "No, I mean it. I'm mad that Dad died. And crying is for babies."

Aunt Dee looked at me, her eyes soft and sad. "I know you think you mean that now, Kevin. But things will look different as time passes."

No.

It wouldn't.

This time Aunt Dee was just plain wrong.

I turned away from her so quickly that I bumped into someone's arm spilling their coffee onto the ugly green rug in the living room. I muttered an apology as I raced to the bathroom, the only room in the house where there was even a little bit of privacy.

Locking the door, I shut out the din of sound. Here in the cool and dim room, I could hear my hoarse breathing. I felt the blood pumping into my head so forcefully I feared I would just explode.

I caught sight of myself in the mirror.

I felt a tidal wave of emotion roar through me.

With a muttered curse, I slammed the soft side of my fist against the mirror over the sink.

With a soft crack, the mirror shattered but remained in place.

Where my face had been just a moment before was now a kaleidoscope of images.

An eye.

Part of my mouth.

An odd looking ear.

Parts of my face were scattered all over: eyes, noses, mouths all stared back at me, dozens and dozens of them and for just a second I almost started crying again, but I remembered my choice.

Anger over sadness.

It just felt better.

Stronger.

The shattered mirror represented the shards of my life, broken and useless now that Dad was gone.

How was I ever going to pick up the pieces of my life?

Dad had been my life.

Yet the pain I felt was a steady reminder that I had no choice but to somehow keep putting one foot in front of the other.

Someway.

Somehow.

I had to learn to live without Dad.

CHAPTER 6

Returning to school was crazy.

I didn't even want to try.

But once I got there, it wasn't as hard as I expected.

While I had seen some of my friends during Dad's rosary, funeral, and reception, they had stuck close by their parents and never came over to talk to me. Even Tony had avoided looking me in the eye when I caught sight of him at the funeral home, and, afterward, he studiously avoided being anywhere near me.

Now, at school, I felt invisible.

Not a single student raised their eyes to meet mine.

My worst fear was that I would start crying the moment someone told me how sorry they were about my Dad.

That had been a total waste of energy.

No one said anything to me.

They didn't greet me.

They didn't say how sorry they were about my dad.

They didn't even look at me.

I'm not sure what was worse, worrying about crying or being ignored.

I never got the chance to compare.

My teachers all made lame overtures when they saw I was back in class. "Welcome back, Kevin," or "Kevin, nice to have you back." I could only give a stiff nod and then curl into my seat, praying for the day to just be over.

Lunch was a lonely affair, but, by that time, I was giving off such ferocious vibes that no one dared to approach me. When the final bell rang, I was exhausted from the effort of holding everything together. I stood by my locker, just staring at my books. I couldn't remember if I had been given any assignments in any of my classes.

I'd been a basket case all day.

"Kevin."

I turned abruptly, hardly believing that someone actually spoke to me. My heart started beating when I saw it was Patty, the girl I had told Dad about the last time I had seen him alive. I'd given her a really nice Valentine, and I still regretted not getting one for Dad. I had to stop myself from staring at her long strawberry blond hair and the sprinkling of freckles across her nose, a testament to her Irish heritage.

She was holding out a red envelope.

A Valentine!

From Patty?

Perhaps this wasn't one of the worst days of my life after all.

"I'm really sorry to hear about your dad." The words I'd been dreading all day long fell from her pink lips. She licked them and then pulled in her bottom lip with her teeth and chewed it nervously. "I'm sorry I didn't have this for you earlier." Then she turned and walked away from me.

I tore into the envelope.

She liked me!

My heart actually liked feeling something different from sorrow. The card wasn't as fancy as the one I'd given her. On the front was the generic "Happy Valentine's Day." I flipped the card open and on the inside it said, "Let's be friends."

Friends?

No!

I didn't want to be friends.

I wanted so much more. I wanted a girlfriend. I wanted someone I could share all these weird and painful emotions with.

Let's be friends was as big an insult as anything my so-called friends threw at me when we played baseball.

I looked up to see Patty moving away from me down the hall. Just then, Tony entered the hall from another corridor and put his arm around Patty's shoulders and her arm fell naturally around his waist.

With a snarl of fury, I threw Patty's Valentine into the trash, grabbed any notebook I could find, slammed the door of my locker, and left the school in the opposite direction. I didn't care that it would take longer to get home. My bruised heart just couldn't take seeing Patty and Tony together.

* * * * *

The days melded into a solid mass of misery.

For the most part my classmates ignored me and I returned the favor, walled away in my grief. My teachers , but they soon started prodding me to participate in class, to turn in my homework and to perform.

They were really pretty nice about it, but I got the message: Life goes on. We're sorry your dad died, but you have to get over it.

So I put in the minimum amount of effort, mainly to keep them off my back. The last thing I needed at this time was for one of them to call Mom for a conference. Ever since Dad died it's like the stuffing got knocked out of her. She moved around the house like a shadow of her former self.

She'd turn the television on and then leave the room, apparently not noticing that shows she hated would come on and play to an empty room. The two drawers in the kitchen where she saved bread bags and strings from the bakery had always been full to overflowing, but now the bags were just stuffed into the drawer instead of being folded neatly. Anytime I had to open the drawer, it would get jammed and I'd have to reach my arm way in the back to remove the jammed plastic, now shredded. From time to time, I'd throw a handful of them away when she wasn't looking just so she could keep saving the new ones.

One Saturday, I decided to organize the kitchen cabinets. Ever since the reception after Dad's funeral, things were put into any cabinet without any thought to organization or placement. I opened all the cabinets and took a few bowls out from between cake mix and cereal boxes. Coffee mugs were mixed side by side juice glasses and cans of fruit cocktail.

I put all the dishes and glasses out on the kitchen table, lining them up in neat piles and rows. Next, I took all the boxes of food out and started tossing some of them into the trash can. She had boxes of pudding that had been expired the past year or two. "They're still good, Kevin. We could eat those or we can give it to someone who will."

"No, Mom! You can't. That's why they have expiration dates on them." It was almost impossible to get my mom to throw things out.

We argued back and forth, but neither of us was really putting any real effort into it. Her objections were token at best. I just pushed on ahead because I had to have some sense of order in my life and dishes and boxes of cereal didn't call me names or throw punches at me.

By the end of the day all the dishes and glasses were back in their place, the food cabinet looked neat and orderly and for once Mom could find her spices if she looked for them.

I took two bags of stale and expired food out to the trash bin where they landed with a thud.

Jeanne was hardly ever home.

She was eighteen, and had a car and a job, which gave her a certain level of independence.

She didn't have to spend time at home any more, something I really envied.

Living with Mom was like living with a ghost.

The only time food tasted any good was when Aunt Dee and Uncle Henry came over. Aunt Dee would take over in the kitchen, cooking up a roasted chicken with mashed potatoes, gravy, fresh vegetables, and angel food cake with frozen strawberries for dessert.

On those days, I could almost believe that Dad was sitting in the front room with Uncle Henry playing cards or cribbage the way they used to.

"Hey, Kevin!"

I turned around to see Tony and Dave across the street waving at me.

"Come on, we're heading over to Joe's house!"

For a moment I hesitated, but having been isolated in my own miserable world the last few weeks, I wanted, no needed, to spend time with my old friends. I could even forgive Tony for catching Patty's eye. I hadn't done anything but admire her from afar. The message in her Valentine just told me she liked me, but I was no one special.

I could live with that.

"Sure. Let me tell my mom." I regretted the words the instant they were out of my mouth, but I couldn't take them back. Besides, I was feeling rather protective of Mom. It only took a few seconds to tell her where I was going and by the smile she gave me, I could see she was happy I was trying to return to a more normal life.

The guys had started walking down the block toward Joe's house, but not so fast I couldn't catch up. I ran through the crisp, spring air, realizing I was happy to be alive.

"Hi!"

Being the boys that they were, they muttered a greeting without looking at me, but I could tell the ice had been broken to some extent.

At least they'd invited me to come over and play with them.

Tony picked up rocks and sticks and tossed them high up into trees at the squirrels, who were scolding and chattering down at us. They could always see it coming and scurried out of the way in time to avoid the missile. I wanted to tell Tony to stop, but being back with some friends felt too good and I didn't want to spoil it. I pushed Dad's words of warning about Tony down. He wasn't throwing anything at cars, and the squirrels were fast enough to stay out of the way, so I figured no harm done.

"So, what are we doing today?"

"We're doin' Fudge's roof today." Tony smirked.

My heart plummeted.

No…not Fudge's roof.

I didn't say anything. I'd been so starved for attention and friendship that it never occurred to me that spending time with Tony and Dave was going to lead to problems… at least not right away.

And a dog can change his spots.

Climbing was not my favorite activities.

I didn't say anything.

I'd found in the weeks since my dad's death that I often could not speak and people simply accepted it: teachers, Mom, my sister, even students in class. It was a trick I'd never used before, but found I rather liked having people not know exactly what I was thinking.

So, I just kept walking and said nothing, was all the time thinking furiously. I'd already seen the tree over Fudge's garage roof, and, unless it had grown about three feet toward the ground since I last saw it, it was still the biggest leap a kid could make and still not get hurt... most of the time. No one had to point out to me I was the most uncoordinated kid in the school.

First, I had to climb the tree, crawl out on the branch over the garage rooftop, and then swing down by my hands and just let go.

It sure sounded easy enough, but I'd been there a few times in the past and not everyone made it.

Fudge's roof was a rite of passage on Dartmouth Street.

Maybe it was time for me to try.

The rest of the way down the street, I just nodded and pretended to hear but not respond to what Tony and Dave were saying.

Inside, I was a quivering mess.

For one thing, I'm terrified of heights, and the thought of climbing a tree over six feet fills me with the kind of fear and dread that would make a grown man cry.

Then, standing on a branch and walking three or four feet out on the branch... who cares if you can hold onto other branches for balance? They're not going to give any kind of support if you fall. They'll rip away in your hands.

Not for the first time in my life did I wonder why my so-called friends didn't respect or honor my fears.

Is it because as a boy, you're not supposed to have fears?

Even Dad had things he was afraid of.

Why should twelve-year-old boys be so certain of the world that they fear nothing?

Long before I was ready, we had reached Mrs. Ursula's back yard and Joe was nowhere to be seen.

I started to wonder if I'd been played.

I wasn't too worried about being in Mrs. Ursula's backyard. She was pretty much blind and deaf and never knew that the neighborhood kids use her yard to access the tree for the Fudge's roof rite of passage. The tree is actually rooted in her back yard.

I like Mrs. Ursula.

She's on my paper route and ever since Dad died, she's given me a dollar a week as a tip. Before, it was a quarter. I know that my increased tips were due to sympathy, but for Mom's sake, I really appreciated the extra money. Once I had enough, I planned to take Mom out to the movies. She and Dad would go once or twice a year, and I figured she'd be missing out on that. But, with my extra tips, I could be the man of the house like Ray said I should and take her to the movies.

When I came back to my surroundings I noticed that Tony and Dave were staring at me.

"What?"

Tony and Dave exchanged a glance.

I could almost read it, "What a retard!"

I maintained my mask of boredom.

"What?" I said again.

"Who's going first?" Dave challenged me.

"You." I snapped back. I figured I could tap into that anger I'd bragged to Aunt Dee about…anger is better than sadness, so anger it was.

He and Tony exchanged glances and then he shrugged.

"Don't matter to me."

With a quick upward jump, Dave grabbed the branch nearest the ground, just above his head and swung his legs upward, under the branch and then over the branch, letting go with his hands. He swung by his knees for a second, his upside-down smile looking de-monic and manic at the same time, his hands sweeping two feet off the ground. He reached up, grabbed the branch with his hands and with a grunt of effort, swung himself upward into a sitting position.

"I'm up!" he shouted.

Tony shushed him with a quick glance back at Mrs. Ursula's kitchen window. I knew she was deaf enough she'd never hear us out there, but I didn't say anything.

Dave was on his feet and climbing up the tree. There were three branches he had to climb before he was at the level of the Fudge Roof Drop. It took him no time to get there, and once he'd reached it, he gave another shout of triumph.

Me, I was feeling sick with fear and I wasn't even the one up in the tree.

I watched, unable to look away.

Why couldn't I do what he was doing? Put one foot in front of the other . . . it was only about four feet away from the trunk of the tree and the branch above looked sturdy enough to hold Dave's weight even if he lost his footing.

Logically, I knew I should be able to do this.

With that thought, I began to visualize myself climbing the tree and walking out on the branch over Fudge's roof.

A wave of optimism rose inside me.

Maybe I could do this today!

If I could, perhaps Tony and Dave would stop pestering me.

It wasn't like the night Tony had chucked a rock at the windshield of the car of the one-armed man. I turned around and glanced at the kitchen window.

Good.

No Mrs. Ursula.

The last thing I wanted to do was scare her by having her see strange shapes in her back yard.

With a whoop of triumph, Dave jumped onto Fudge's roof and did a few steps like a football player who catches a touchdown pass. Then he ran over to the side and flung himself over the edge, holding onto the roof with his hands. He let go and managed the two-foot drop with great aplomb.

My heart dropped into my stomach.

I'd changed my mind.

There was absolutely no way I could do this.

Tony was already leaping up for the branch and was soon swinging by his knees just as Dave had done. I watched and he followed exactly in Dave's footsteps, up the tree, across the branch, down onto the roof, and then back to the ground. From across the fence, now, the two were high-fiving one another, and then looked at me expectantly.

It was now or never.

I walked over to the tree and stood underneath.

I looked up. The branch that Dave and Tony had managed to grab seemed about twenty feet in the air. I closed my eyes and jumped, hands outstretched and I managed to jam my middle finger on the branch.

With a muffled oath, I jumped again, this time with my eyes open, and, to my surprise, I reached the branch and was hanging by my fingertips.

I felt exultant.

I didn't think I would even make it this far.

"Hey, way to go, Kevin!"

Tony's shout of encouragement made me swell with pride. Maybe things would be different after all.

I swung from my hands as I had watched the two of them and used the momentum of my body to swing my legs up and over the branch.

Again, success.

I let go with my hands and whooped as they had done, swinging from my knees.

Then things went wrong.

I reached back up with my hands to swing my entire body upward, but somehow misjudged where I was, and, for a moment, I was airborne and then collided with the ground with great force. I landed on the back of my neck and upper back. It knocked the wind out of me and for a few moments I thought I'd broken my neck.

I couldn't breathe.

I couldn't move.

Long afterward, I wondered why I had expected Dave and Tony to come over and see if I was OK. Instead they laughed at my stupidity and just walked away.

The sun shone through the bare branches of the tree that had betrayed me in Mrs. Ursula's back yard. It mocked me as surely as the sound of Dave's and Tony's voices moving down the block away from me.

What an idiot I was to think I could manage the challenge of Fudge's roof. I was even more of an idiot to believe that Tony, my supposed friend, would have changed and been concerned for my welfare.

* * * * *

The next Monday, I arrived at school before the morning bell, hoping to somehow redeem myself.

Great!

I'd arrived just as they were choosing teams for baseball. I ran up to the guys, hoping to be chosen soon.

I really didn't care if they chose me first because they pitied me because of my dad.

I just wanted to be chosen.

Slowly the teams were formed and I stood there, still waiting to be called. Then, the absolute worst thing I could have imagined happened. The boy standing next to me got picked and then the team captain of the next choice team turned away and said, "All right... let's play ball!"

He'd completely ignored me.

It was bad enough to have been chosen last, but I hadn't even been picked this time.

I felt a rage begin to simmer inside of me.

Fortunately, the school bell rang just moments later because I don't know what I would have done if it hadn't.

The story of my fall at Fudge's roof had obviously made its way to school.

Once again, I was a total failure.

CHAPTER 7

Usually, when a box arrived at our house, I was the first one to insist we open it.

Since Dad died, I'd pretty much lost my desire for anything new.

A box had been delivered yesterday. It was a very large box that held the look of great promise, and, at first I was a bit interested. Then, as I fingered the label, wondering what could be inside, I noted the New Hampshire return address.

From my Aunt Chris.

Uh-oh.

This could be good or bad.

My cousin George was just a little older than me and Aunt Chris knew what it was like to need clothes for kids, after all she had thirteen kids. This box was probably for me and full of George's cast-off clothes. It might have some cast-off toys as well, but the likelihood was in favor of clothes.

Great.

Hand-me-downs.

My favorite.

Not.

I wouldn't be nagging mom to open that any time soon.

Outside it was a wet, gray April Saturday. I'd begun to live for the weekends where I could stay in my pajamas until noon on Saturday, and, today was just perfect. The weather matched my mood.

Jeanne was already gone, probably working or hanging out with her friends. The six years difference in our ages never seemed as big as it did now. Since Dad's death, she had been spending less and less time at home.

Part of me welcomed the quiet.

My mother puttered around in her bedroom, not knowing I was awake yet. I ambled into the kitchen where I poured myself a bowl of Cheerios and opened the sugar container. The silver top clanked against the white ceramic body.

I paused a moment, listening intently to see if Mom had heard.

With great stealth, I spooned four, then five heaping spoonfuls of sugar over my cereal. I loved that mass of melted sugar at the bottom of the bowl, and without supervision from Mom or my sister, it was going to be a great big gooey mess today.

I added a little milk, and then I shuffled into the living room where I turned on cartoons and sat on my old and very well loved Pan-Am sleeping bag.

Up until the time Dad died, I'd wanted to be a pilot.

Now, I didn't want to be much of anything.

I just wanted the pain in the center of my chest to go away.

Just as the Roadrunner bested Wiley Coyote and I was scooping up the last of the sugary milk, Mom came into the room with the big box. "Kevin, I'm glad you're up. We need to go through this box of clothes Chris just sent."

My least favorite activity on any given day was trying on clothes. Today just didn't feel like a day to try on someone else's clothes. Maybe I could put it off a week or two or thirty.

"Do I have to?"

Mom frowned, something she was doing a lot lately. I really missed her ready smile and the way she was always there to help with anything. Now, it seemed like everything she did was a huge effort.

"Yes, we have to. Look at how much time it must have taken Chris to pack all this, to say nothing of how much it must have cost to ship it!" She flipped the lid of the box over to see the cost of shipping.

By her pursed lips, I could tell it was a lot.

I knew Mom was struggling to keep things together for Jeanne and me. Most of the time, I didn't think about how hard it must be for her until someone gave us charity. I think she could take just about anything except charity, and, yet, we were in no position to turn down clothing.

Just last Sunday, I'd put on my clothes for church and when I came out of the room, Mom had put her hand to her mouth in horror. "Kevin! Are those your newest pants?"

"Yeah, why?"

"They're halfway to your knees!"

My growth spurts had put a crimp in the budget.

I decided to give her a break. It wasn't her fault she couldn't keep buying me new pants. "Fine, I'll try them on."

It was just easier this way.

I also knew if I didn't, she'd go down the guilt trip road and I was not in the mood for that.

She pulled out a couple of shirts that looked to be okay, and I picked up one that looked promising and put it on after shedding my pajama shirt.

That should make her happy.

Mom looked at me critically, and nodded. "That looks good." She started sifting through and putting pants on the back of the chair;, I knew she was looking for pants that were long enough to fit my ever-lengthening legs.

"Here," she held out a pair of pants, "try these on. They look long enough."

I backed away from her in horror.

"No way!"

She had to be kidding!

They were PINK!

I'd be the laughing stock of all the neighborhood.

"Come on, Kevin. Right now."

"Ma, they're pink."

"They are not."

"Yes, they are too!" By now my voice was rising, becoming shrill.

"Kevin, they're red, just a little faded because George has worn them before. Now put them on." This time, both her face and voice were hard. There was no emotion. I could tell she was holding it back. The only time she cried was when she was alone in her room late at night. I'd listen through the thick darkness of the house, and I cried with her, both of us alone in our beds.

I stomped to my room, threw off my pajamas and pulled the pants on.

Great.

They fit perfectly.

Disgusted, I stomped back out into the living room where Mom waited, still going through the box, putting shirts, pants, and underwear and socks in separate piles.

She had to see this would never work.

"Kevin! Those look really good on you!" She smiled.

I just stared at her.

Couldn't she see what was going to happen?

"I don't like them."

"They're perfect. Now you're going to wear them today and that's final."

We continued to argue.

I never paid attention to Mom's "that's final" argument. Since Dad died, I'd become a lot more argumentative. Mom still always bested me, because I really couldn't stand to hurt her. But, come on, why would I want to wear clothes someone else had worn? And pink? I was having some serious doubts about my cousin. Any self-respecting guy did not wear pink pants.

"Kevin, go on outside. The rain's stopped. These can be your play clothes; you don't have to wear them at school."

With that pronouncement, she picked up the clothes that were the right size, marched into my room, and began putting my cousin's hand-me-downs into my bureau drawers. And, to make matters worse, she started taking out some of the clothes that were my favorites.

"No! Don't take that shirt!" This time I yelled at her; I couldn't help it.

I grabbed the shirt she held in her hands and hugged it close to me. It was the shirt I wore the last time I went to see Dad in the hospital. I usually had the shirt hidden under my pillow, but because I hadn't made my bed, it was just lying there in plain sight.

Mom stopped and without saying anything she gently took the shirt from me and put it back down on the bed. I breathed a silent breath of relief. She still felt guilty about not waking me up the night Dad died, so this is where I had power over her.

When she spoke, her voice was a little thick and hoarse, "Fine, I won't take that shirt. But I want you to outside and get some exercise. You've been eating too much sugar and watching too much TV."

Great.

Now that Dad was gone she was going to nag me about my health habits.

I couldn't take it anymore, so I slammed out the front door and sat on the steps to the sidewalk.

My eyes caught movement across the street.

Crap.

If I'd seen them, I wouldn't have been so quick to escape the house. Usually I looked both directions before leaving my front door.

This time, I was ambushed.

There they were, the whole gang: Tony, Dave, Derek, Tommy, and the rest. And it didn't take long for them to notice. As they crossed the street coming toward me, Tony struck a pose, just like the new Docker's commercial, "Nice pants, Kev!"

The guys all laughed.

That was it.

I knew they'd zeroed in on the one thing that hurt me the most today.

"Hey, when did pink become the new studly color?"

"Hey Kev, how'd you like a pink jacket to go with your girly pants?"

Their voices blended into a cacophony of sound swirling around in my head.

I tried to shut it out.

In that split second, my head felt like it was going to explode.

I looked up and met Tony's eyes. Silently I pleaded with him to just leave me alone. All those years of friendship had to mean something. For a brief second, I thought he might call the mob off, but that flicker of compassion was so brief and fleeting, I probably just imagined it. Instead he shouted, "Hey, maybe these pants wouldn't look so gay if they were a different color!"

"Yeah!"

"Let's do it!"

I started to get up to run inside the house. I didn't care how chicken it looked, but then Dave and Derek grabbed my arms, swung me around, and it was Tony who landed the first punch to my gut.

"Oof!"

I gagged.

I couldn't breathe.

Doubled over, I struggled to think of a way out, but within seconds strong hands grabbed my wrists and ankles and carried me to the street, to the deep depression in the road right in front of my house, the one I jumped over every day to and from school.

But today, because of the heavy rain, it was one big, murky puddle.

"One, two, three!" They let go and I crashed into the puddle. Old leaves, decayed after the winter, stuck to my eyes. In a panic, I flailed to get my head out of the water. I knew I got some of the guys wet as they yelled in protest.

I blinked frantically and choked out some of the frigid, muddy water.

They circled me like a pack of dogs, feigning attack, and laughing at the sorry picture I made sitting in the puddle of water that totally covered my legs.

"See, no more pink pants, Kev!"

"Yeah! Now they're brown."

"Nah, they're the color of MUD!"

Furious, I scrambled to my feet and charged.

I didn't care who I hit, but I was determined to hit someone. In my blind rage, I didn't see the punch, but I sure felt it, and over I went, this time I was on my stomach and several shoes pummeled me in the sides and rained down on my shoulders and arms as I raised my hands to protect my head and face.

"Let's do it again!"

With even more violence, hands grabbed my wrists and ankles, but this time I really struggled. I fought as hard as I could, screaming and writhing like a wild thing until someone, I think it was Derek, grabbed my hair and jerked my head back.

He put his face next to my ear and growled, "Keep fighting you little piss-ant and you'll never walk again."

I felt my insides turn to liquid, he sounded like he meant it. This time, because I was face first, I saw the puddle coming.

And it came fast.

I didn't have enough time to take a breath, because my face was already under water when I inhaled. In total panic, I thrust myself up with my hands and coughed, gagged, and choked, puking up muddy water, feeling it burn down my throat and up into my sinuses.

I got the cold feeling of fear inside my chest.

These guys had crossed some kind of line today.

In a panic, I pushed myself up and tried to run, but I was surrounded.

Again and again, they picked me up and threw me into the puddle. Once I hit my head on the edge of the sidewalk, my vision spun and I saw stars, and for a moment the world went black, but it was only just a moment.

My one-time friends had turned into a frenzied pack of wild animals and I was their terrified prey.

I learned to not get up.

If they wanted to throw me into the puddle, they would have to work for it by picking me up out of the puddle themselves. The first time I didn't fight, I just lay there, eyes closed, feeling the cold texture of the roadway underneath my bruised cheek. Grit and mud had worked their way underneath my clothes, and I felt limp and breathless.

I thought I was dying, but my body continued to fight to live by gasping great big gulps of air. It was the only sound I could hear and then I heard them coming back at me with grunts, and growls, and snarls.

This time, they decided to cover me with mud and leaves. They were all covered with muddy water by this time, so they no longer cared if they got dirty. I felt each donation of rotting vegetation land on my body and felt like I was being buried alive. At first I just lay there in surrender until they started to bury my head.

That's when I discovered something; I still had plenty of will to live.

With a roar of rage I clambered to my feet and rushed at the first boy in sight. It happened to be Tony. I rushed him and tackled him by the waist, swinging us both around with the momentum of my fury and we both landed in the puddle. I felt a certain amount of satisfaction at his grunt of pain, but Tony's friends quickly extinguished my momentary triumph.

They threw me into the puddle again, piled all the collected debris onto me and then, with their feet, kicked at me, holding me down, and began pushing my face under water.

"That's enough."

I barely heard the words, my ears were so full of mud and water, but the vicious hands that were vices let me go, some more quickly than others.

"Tony, you're an ass. He's had enough. Leave him alone."

It was Tony's older brother, Mark.

I'd seen Mark plenty of times, but because he was older, I had never spent any time around him.

I was just grateful the attack was over.

My tormentors left me, slinging insults with venom and making threats for a dismal future.

As their laughter faded, I just lay there.

I wasn't sure how much time passed.

Maybe part of me hoped a car would just come along Dartmouth Street and take me away from this life. I felt weary and hollow inside with an emptiness that I doubted could ever be filled.

In that moment, I realized I hated my life and everyone in it.

Dad had always said, "Just punch them in the nose," when I told him about being bullied. And while I had one moment as I charged Tony, when I recalled his words, I realized I just wasn't that kind of person.

I didn't want to hurt people.

I didn't want to inflict pain.

For a twelve-year-old, I'd endured enough pain already for a lifetime. And if I had to inflict pain on someone just to be able to live in peace, well then, maybe I didn't want to be in this world.

I rolled over onto my back.

My injuries began to throb, and my laboring heart began to slow and settle into a comforting thrub, thrub, thrub. I could feel my breathing return to normal.

I was cold, wet, and shaking with emotion.

With a disgusted sigh, I opened my eyes and saw the dark sky gathering behind the naked branches of the great elm tree far above my head. Little buds were just barely noticeable and they offered no protection from the rain that began to fall again.

I didn't care.

I wanted the rain to wash the humiliation of my hideous attack from my memory.

A shadow leaned over me.

I felt a momentary flash of terror, until I realized it was our war-crazy neighbor, Dean. He walked with a cane, and never said a word to anyone. He and my dad would exchange brief greetings anytime they met out front on the sidewalk, but no one else in the neighborhood ever did.

Normally, I would have been terrorized to be this close to Dean.

After today, I didn't think I could ever be afraid again.

He reached out a hand to me, and gritting my teeth against the pain, I accepted his help. I couldn't bring myself to look him in the eyes. The last thing I wanted or needed was someone's pity.

Maybe he just didn't want me to get squashed by the next car that came down our street.

"Go on inside, son." His voice was gruff, but the hands that pushed me toward the steps I had so reluctantly descended twenty minutes before were exquisitely gentle.

I mumbled, "Thanks," and trudged up the steps, leaving a wet trail of mud, leaves, and grief in my wake.

I blinked muddy water and gathering tears from my eyes as I stood before the door of my house, listening to the pattering of water coming off my clothes. I drew in a big breath, opened the door and headed straight for the bathroom where I pulled off my shoes, shirt, and those hated pink pants. I was shivering so hard by this time from both emotion and the cold that it was a struggle to get the pants off. It was as if they had developed a life of their own and clung to me, like some perverse symbiotic relationship. Finally I kicked them away from me and stood under the hottest shower I could stand washing every bit of grime off my body.

Even when I was clean, I stood under the hot spray.

Perhaps I was trying to eliminate the target that had somehow become tattooed on my body, the tattoo that seemed to say, "Hit me!"

My anger against Tony began simmering beneath the surface.

He had dominated me throughout our entire friendship.

Until now I had accepted it as part of his personality.

It was the price I paid for his friendship.

He was a jock, a natural at any sport he tried. I pretty much sucked at sports, and I knew it. It hadn't really seemed to matter much. We would play baseball, and I would strike out or miss a fly ball. The guys would razz me a bit and say having me on their team was like having no one, but I'd been able to take it because I was part of the group.

The water hammered my skull, and, a deep, intense anger took hold in my heart.

What Tony had done today was total betrayal, and it hurt like nothing else I'd ever experienced except my dad's death.

As I stood there, I realized it felt exactly like a death.

Tony and I had been friends since we were four years old, sleeping over at one another's houses, going to the beach, the pool, and playing Big Jim, McHale's Navy on Tony's back porch, and Battleship. I had done nothing but be his faithful friend all these years.

And today, when all I needed was him to just stand up for me a little. I would even have taken a few punches if it meant we could still be friends, but this total humiliation was it.

I had no Dad.

I had no friends.

What was there to live for now?

Finally, all the hot water was used, and I had to get out of the shower. I wrapped myself in a towel and tromped back to my room and put my pajamas back on.

If Mom hadn't made me put those stupid pants on, none of this would have happened.

She was waiting for me when I came back out, a sad and confused look in her eyes. "What happened?"

"What do you think? They didn't like my pink pants."

And with that, I grabbed the stinking, soggy, pink mass from the bathroom, shook it at my mother, mindless of the mess I was leaving on the floor, and stormed into the kitchen where I threw them into the trash can. "I'm never wearing those disgusting pants again! I can't believe you did this to me! You must hate me!" I was screaming now, out of control.

Mom moved closer and tried to hug me, "Kev, I'm sorry. They're just being boys."

At this I jerked away from her, a vitriolic mixture of anger and fear boiling inside me. As I pulled away, I looked straight at her and what I saw was my own undoing. The raw, searing pain in her own eyes defused my anger and I started to cry. This time when she reached for me, I crumpled into her arms and for a few minutes we both cried, this time together.

I cried the tears that had been building up since Dad died.

I cried because he wasn't there to tell me that tomorrow would be better.

I cried because he loved me no matter what, and he didn't care if I couldn't play sports or that I couldn't run as fast as everyone else, and he certainly wouldn't have cared if I had worn pink pants. He would have put his hand on my neck, cradled my head and looked me in the eyes and said, "Nothing matters but you Kevin. I love you no matter what."

But he was no longer here to reassure me.

I missed his warm presence and his loving guidance. I missed our special Saturday times together. I was sure if my dad had lived, today would have never happened.

And I cried because suddenly childhood seemed like a big fake-out.

It is supposed to be about puppies and games and fun. About friendships, baseball, and good times.

When Mom handed me a tissue, I wiped my eyes and blew my nose.

I felt like my blinders had been removed from my eyes.

This was nothing but a big fat ugly world.

As Mom cleaned up the mess of leaves and mud I made when I shook the sodden bundle at her, I curled up in my sleeping bag in Dad's big yellow-brown armchair, feeling its warmth as if they were his arms surrounding me, comforting me.

The rest of the day it rained and I pretended my dad would be home shortly and we would watch *Creature Double Feature*, and that everything would once again be back to normal.

I dozed fitfully, waking every now and again, feeling the physical pain of my bruises, and the deep-seated rawness of my grief.

Finally my weary, aching body let go and I dropped into a sleep too dark and too silent for dreams to interrupt.

CHAPTER 8

For the remainder of the school year, I became Mr. Invisible.

I skulked down the halls, one shoulder almost touching the lockers so that I only had to watch out for one flank, not both. I still got bumped a lot more than most kids, sending my books and papers flying. Each time, I would just wait until that particular tormentor moved on and then I would pick up my mess of torn papers with footprint marks all over them.

My teachers noticed I was turning in less than pristine homework, yet, they never said anything. I paid only enough attention in class to not get called on, and when a teacher did call on me, I would mumble an answer. My homeroom teacher stuck it out the longest, asking me to repeat myself until she could finally hear me, but by the end of May I had worn her down to the point she seemed relieved to pass me along to the next grade where I would be someone else's problem.

The first day of summer vacation used to be one of my favorite days of the year.

The summer of 1979 saw images of our Revere Beach outings, the MDC Big pool, and picking ruby red raspberries from Little Mr. Sicily's garden, go down the toilet.

It was the summer of guerrilla warfare.

Dartmouth Street was the war zone.

Every morning when I looked out during the scorching hot days, I had two questions.

"How are we going to survive without Dad?"

And "Who will torture or embarrass me today?"

When the guys from the neighborhood came by, calling out for me, taunting, even pounding on the door, I ignored them, hiding behind the curtains and willing them to just leave me in peace.

At least at school I was a target only between classes when no teachers were in the hallways. Now that summer was here, I didn't even have the relative safety that had provided.

"Kevin, it's a nice day. Go outside and play." Mom nagged me to get up from Dad's chair where I was slumped watching cartoons. I couldn't explain to her how I felt close to Dad just by sitting in his chair. She had to work from eight in the morning until two in the afternoon, and she made it her job in the morning to see to it that I didn't sit in front of the TV all day.

I still had my paper route, and, fortunately, the summer route was even earlier than in the winter, so I still left the house before the sun was up and if I hurried through my route, I was finished long before any kids in my neighborhood had finished breakfast and ventured outside. That early morning paper route was my sanity for a time because I felt it was the only time I felt truly safe. No one was there to push me, poke me, call me names or worse. I spoke to no one, except the few early workers who were leaving at dawn, and that was usually just a greeting or a wave of the hand.

Once I got home and Mom left for work, I was at a loss.

I had plenty of models to work on, but they brought too many memories of Dad, I couldn't face working on them alone.

I was pretty much past the stage of playing Big Jim, even though I still admired his musculature and wished one day to be just like him and chop a block of wood in half.

Reading reminded me too much of school.

As for playing with the kids in the neighborhood, it wasn't worth the hassle.

My anger at Tony simmered underneath the surface, becoming a white hot heat that threatened to overpower me. Why was it that my supposed friend since we were four years old had decided to become such a bully toward me? The first few weeks after Dad died, the bullying incidents stopped; but, once they started up again, it was like they were making up for lost time.

I would hear their voices playing in the street after dusk as I sat in a chair by the window in the dark watching them, wishing things could be different. I finally figured out that groups of people always seem to have one in the group they had to pick on, and I had been that one. For a long time, I'd put up with it because the teasing hadn't really been all that bad. But once they crossed the line, the day they kept throwing me in the puddle, it was like I had somehow been marked and everyone knew they could pick on me, tease me, and bully me.

It was no use talking to Mom about it. She worked as a secretary for the truant officer, and, to her, what I was going through was just normal rough-housing.

She knew about the puddle incident, but she hadn't seen it happen. I'm pretty sure she thought I was exaggerating.

I hadn't bothered to tell her how bad things had gotten at school. I always wondered if any of my teachers had ever said anything to her about my dirty and torn homework papers. They probably felt sorry for me about my dad, and didn't want to burden her with any problems.

I wasn't causing trouble, so they kept quiet.

* * * * *

My thirteenth birthday arrived. While, I'd managed to numb my pain about Dad dying in regard to everyday things, this was one event I couldn't stuff down into a deep enough or dark enough place that it wouldn't trouble me.

Mom looked at me at breakfast and said brightly, "Shall we get your cake from Elm Street Bakery like we did last year?"

I just looked at her.

"Come on, Kevin. You turn thirteen today. We can get you a cake, and, if you like, we can go to the Brown Jug for pizza tonight."

My throat was really tight and at first I couldn't talk so I swallowed hard. "I'm not celebrating my birthday."

"Sure you are."

"No. I am not."

"Listen, I know it's really hard, but Kevin, your dad would want you to celebrate," and with that she got up from the table, picked up the phone and dialed the number for the bakery. I listened to her order my favorite cake, chocolate fudge.

I shook my head.

I wasn't going to eat it.

She could buy a hundred cakes.

I wasn't ever going to eat cake again.

Leaving my cereal bowl on the kitchen table, I slouched into the living room, turned on the television and sat in Dad's chair and gave myself over to missing him. Maybe I had tried too hard to be tough. Perhaps if I let myself miss having him around it wouldn't be so hard. For the first time in weeks, I cried just a little bit, but everything that had happened since the funeral had toughened me so much, I found no relief in crying.

It just made me feel hot and miserable.

The only thing that would make me feel better was having my dad back, and that sure wasn't going to happen.

Mom stood in the kitchen doorway for a couple of minutes, watching me. I could see her out of the corner of my eye, but I just ignored her. Pretty soon she went to her room to get ready for work. At least, she wasn't going to give me any grief today about watching television all day.

I should have a birthday every day.

I passed the time the day I turned thirteen dozing in Dad's chair, watching mindless garbage on TV, and sitting by the window watching people go about their business on Dartmouth Street.

How could life just keep going on?

I thought my entire world had stopped when Dad died, yet things just keep moving.

People's lives move right along.

Mom's.

Jeanne's.

Mine.

No matter how I tried to stop everything; stop caring, stop doing things, the world just wouldn't let me. About an hour before Mom was due home, I went outside after carefully scoping things out to make sure Tony or Dave weren't out there waiting to pounce on me.

I trotted over to Elm Street and then over to the cemetery.

I found Dad's grave without too much difficulty.

Even the grass had kept right on growing.

Dad's grave was no longer a brown dirt rectangle. It was covered with beautiful green grass, and there were fresh flowers lying next to his headstone. I wondered who had brought them. It had to have been today; they still looked very fresh.

I stood there, listening to the wind high in the tall trees of the cemetery. Some people find it too creepy spending time in a cemetery, but I kind of liked it.

"Dad," I whispered, "can you hear me?"

What was I thinking?

Of course he couldn't hear me.

He was dead.

And yet, there was a part of me that wasn't altogether convinced he couldn't hear me. Somehow I felt closer to Dad here than anywhere else, except perhaps in his chair.

I knew if Mom caught me talking to Dad in his chair, she would take me to a shrink for sure.

"So, how long does it take to grow up and be someone like you? Huh, Dad? Everyone liked you, admired you, heck they even looked forward to you coming, knowing full well you were going to give them grief for something or the other. I can't even walk down the hallway at school without some character punching me in the gut, knocking my books out of my hands or tripping me in the cafeteria."

I sat down and crossed my legs.

Time to ask some tough questions.

"What does a guy have to do to get some respect? People really respected you and you were never mean to them. I tried to be a good friend to Tony and now all he does is put me down and punch me. He makes other people laugh by playing tricks on me. My life sucks, Dad!"

By closing my eyes just a little, I could picture my dad sitting right in front of me, his warm eyes focused intently on me. No one in my life paid that kind of attention to me right now.

Jeanne didn't.

She was trying to figure out how to be an adult at eighteen.

Mom couldn't.

I knew it took everything she had to just get out of bed in the morning to go to work.

Auntie Dee and Uncle Henry were pretty close, but they had their own problems.

"It's just me, now, Dad. I don't know how to do it. I needed you to help me figure out how to grow up." My voice broke at that point and I cried for the second time that day.

This time it was a little easier.

I could almost imagine my dad's arms coming around me and just holding me, letting me get it out of my system. He never thought less of me if I showed any kind of weakness like crying.

He never felt that I wasn't living up to his name when I was always picked last for baseball or softball. He was proud of me no matter what.

I could just about hear him say, "Kevin, I love you no matter what. You're my kid. Why wouldn't I be proud of you?"

"How am I going to do it, Dad? How can I find my way without you?"

The sound of that question echoed through the trees, and then left me with just the whisper of the breeze for an answer. I would have to find my own way.

"Thanks, Dad. Maybe I'll see you tomorrow."

I promised myself from that day on, unless I was out of town, I would go and talk to my Dad in the cemetery every day. I needed some connection with Dad, and this was it.

* * * * *

Back at the house, I got home after Mom had arrived from work. Her face looked worried until she saw me and then its frown lines eased into a relieved smile. "So, you're home."

"Yeah. I went for a walk."

"Good. I'm glad you went outside for a bit. Did you see anyone?" What she was really asking me was if I had done anything with the neighborhood kids.

Not likely.

"No, I didn't see anyone. I just walked." I don't know why I didn't tell her I'd gone to see Dad at the cemetery. Maybe it would freak her out. Although, the more I thought about it, the more it made sense the flowers I had found there had come from her.

"I got your cake."

My sigh was loud enough for her to hear. "I told you not to."

"Well, Auntie Dee and Uncle Henry are coming over. We'll just have sandwiches and cake here since you don't feel like going out tonight."

That was an okay compromise. I really didn't want to go out, but having my aunt and uncle over wasn't a problem.

"Is there anyone else you want to invite?"

I didn't even bother to answer that question and walked out of the kitchen.

Who was she kidding?

Who would I invite?

Every friend I ever had had turned into either a moron or a bully. No, I was as friendless as a kid could get. But, I wasn't going to feel sorry for myself again today.

My talk with Dad had helped me a little bit.

Dinner with Mom, Jeanne, and my aunt and uncle turned out fine. I kept wishing I could see Dad just once more and that's what I wished when Mom made me blow out the candles on my cake. I still refused to eat the cake. Even when I saw the pain in Mom's eyes, I just couldn't do it.

Birthdays had always been special in our family.

I was thirteen today.

So what.

I was also fatherless.

Why would I eat cake?

Mom gave me a box to open.

"Mom, I said no cake and definitely no presents."

She looked at me steadily, still holding out the small box. "I think you'll want to open this one." Her voice let me know I wasn't going to get out of opening the gift, so with little grace and no gratitude, I grabbed it out of her hands and pulled the ribbon and wrapping off tossing it to the floor to show my contempt.

My breathing stopped when I opened the box. Inside were some of Dad's tie-tacks, his cuff-links, and his white gold wedding band. They swam before my eyes as I teared up yet again that day.

What could I say now?

I'd been a total ass to my mom.

I cleared my throat once.

Twice.

Then I muttered, "Thank you."

I couldn't stop looking at my gift. I hadn't wanted anything for my birthday, but I sure wasn't going to turn this one down.

Auntie Dee, pretending there was nothing wrong pressed another small package into my hand. "Here, Kevin. Open this one too."

Still numb with emotion, I opened her gift and saw a gold chain necklace.

I looked up at her in some confusion. "We figured you couldn't wear your dad's ring on your hand yet, but you could wear it on this."

Together we strung Dad's ring onto the gold necklace and then she fastened it at the back of my neck. It was just long enough I could hide the ring beneath the collar of my shirt.

"Thank you. It's perfect."

I couldn't think of anything else to say.

This really was the perfect gift for me on this miserable day. I couldn't have Dad back, but perhaps my wish had come true to some extent; I had one of my dearest mementos of him.

Right up against my heart.

Two weeks after my birthday, I was invited to stay with my cousins. They had invited me to stay with them shortly after Dad's death, but I didn't want to leave Mom and my sister. I felt like our little family had already shrunk enough, so I'd turned down the invitation.

This time, however, I welcomed the opportunity.

Being with my cousins meant a total reprieve.

They were family.

They loved me.

And I wouldn't have to constantly look over my shoulder to see if someone was sneaking up or ganging up on me.

To be able to eat, play, and sleep without the constant feeling of paranoia that had become my constant companion was a very welcome respite.

After I returned from my two week stay at my cousin's house, my halcyon time was over.

For all I knew, Tony and Dave and the rest of their gang had been banging on our front door, shouting insults the whole time I had been gone.

Ha! The joke was on them.

I hadn't been there.

For the rest of the summer, my daily routine was to get up, deliver my papers, eat breakfast, watch TV, visit Dad at the cemetery, and then walk the three miles to Mom's office reaching it right about lunchtime.

During my walk, I would go with the stealth of a ninja, avoiding any place I could be trapped.

Every day was a new challenge to me to avoid the bullying in my little piece of the planet. On these walks I was desperate to find things that might be good luck charms, something that would hopefully change my daily struggle.

Most days, I'd wear one of Dad's necktie pins or cuff links like a security blanket. To me, it felt like there was good energy in these mementos from Dad.

All I had was hope and faith, and, I hoped and prayed that carrying these good luck charms would change my daily outcome.

As I walked, my mind wandered, and I invited in any opportunity to find beauty in the world, but it felt as if my life's canvas had been erased or even worse, painted black.

When I arrived at Mom's office, she looked up and smiled at me. "Hi Kevin, you're just in time to go get us some lunch." I knew we didn't have a whole lot of money, but she handed me a couple bucks and had me go get a slice of pizza and fries from Papa Gino's over in Everett square.

She let me bring the food back to her office, which was nice.

It let me continue to avoid the world.

I avoided the bullies.

But I also avoided meeting new people because my 13-year-old brain would leap to "How is this person going to humiliate me?"

I know it sounds like I was suspicious of the world, and that's probably not a very healthy place to be. But in my mind, any place I was alone wasn't safe.

Back at Mom's office, we set out the pizza and fries and ate together. Mom had stopped asking how my days were going because it was pretty much the same answer, "Okay, I guess."

I'd told her about how the neighborhood kids would come up to the door and shout things at me because they knew I was home alone, and she'd just give me her standard response, "They're just being kids. You should go out and play with them."

Right.

And I should just jump into a river full of piranha too.

Dad had been my confidante, the one whom I shared all my fears and dreams. With him, I could bare my soul and he never looked at me as if I were somehow lacking.

Mom, on the other hand, looked at me as if something were wrong with me.

She held me.

She comforted me.

But she was totally at a loss when it came to helping me figure out how to be a normal boy in this jungle of life. So my life became a boring parade of the same things.

Each afternoon, when we pulled up to the house, I would think, "Good, now it's only a few hours until dinner and bed; maybe tomorrow will be a better day."

That summer was the longest of my life.

I never doubted Mom's love for me.

I didn't want to play ball.

Why would I?

I sucked at it and everyone knew it.

Each time, Mom suggested I only spend time with the neighborhood boys if they were playing an organized game. "They won't pick on you then; you'll all be too busy. Right?"

She just didn't get it.

She didn't understand that it would be a game where more shame and guilt would be heaped on me because I couldn't hit or catch the ball.

But I never said anything.

She didn't understand.

She couldn't understand.

Mom had absolutely no idea how much growing up for a boy was like living among savages.

All she could do was give me her "boys will be boys" speech, or tell me to explain to my persecutors how much their actions bothered me.

She had no idea that "using my words" virtually guaranteed I'd be permanently branded an idiot. While Dad had suggested I just "punch them in the nose," advice I couldn't follow any more than Mom's, at least he had claimed to understand what I was facing.

When he was alive, this gave me some comfort.

I figured I'd learn from Dad as I navigated the shark-infested waters of being a boy in my neighborhood. I did not have the necessary tools to deal with this at my age. Who did? I'd been the center of my dad's world and he was the center of mine. Now the one person I depended on for guidance was gone and I didn't know where to turn.

I was a nice boy—everyone would say that—so why was this happening to me?

I went to church.

I prayed.

And nothing helped.

I just wanted to fit in and get along. But my hatred toward my bullies grew daily. Deep down, I knew the searing hot anger was a very negative emotion, but I didn't know how to get past it.

I worried what would happen when I finally let it loose.

The weekend before school started, I asked Mom if there was anything I could do to earn a little extra spending money.

"Sure, Kevin. I was planning on painting the back porch. I have the paint all ready, and you know where the brushes are."

Mom was relieved I wanted to do something other than sit in front of the TV all day. I got the paintbrushes, remembering the last time they'd been used on the front porch. I'd helped Dad paint the front porch almost exactly a year before.

Mom met me on the back porch with two cans of paint.

"Here you go. This should be plenty to get the job done."

She hovered for a few minutes, watching me open one can of gray paint and then carefully stir it with the wooden stir stick just as Dad had shown me. Once she was satisfied I knew what I was doing, she said, "OK, well, I'll be inside if you need me."

I started at the back door, knowing I needed to get that painted first so it would be dry by the time anyone wanted to come out. There is something really therapeutic about painting. You have a worn, tired piece of wood that has definitely seen better days and cover it with a coat of paint and immediately it looks better, brighter, and almost as if it were new again.

I wondered if there might be a way to paint over my life.

The job was about half done when I realized I had an audience.

Great.

Don Blaylock was watching me work.

I ignored him as well as I could. Part of me just wanted to say, "Hi Don, how's it going?" We used to be real good friends a few years back. We both made airplane models and had spent hours side by side working on our models together. But then something changed and I became the target for every bully in the neighborhood. It was no longer cool for people like Don to hang out with me.

As I kept working, I could tell Don's intentions weren't good. This was not a friendly house call; there was going to be some level of humiliation involved in it for me. Word around the neighborhood was that Don got abused at home, and I got the sense his dad would take a belt to him when he got out of line. Mr. Blaylock was an intimidating man, six feet tall and a couple hundred pounds of pure muscle topped by a handlebar mustache. Mr. Blaylock had always treated me very well whenever I was over at Don's house, yet I know he could be pretty hard on his son.

Today it looked like Don intended to take his frustrations out on me.

"Hey, Moron, where'd ya learn to paint?"

I continued painting, trying harder and harder to ignore him. Cursing under my breath at my own stupidity. Why had I agreed to do a chore that put me outside this long? I painted another plank, focusing completely on covering the wood while mentally willing him to leave me in peace.

Unfortunately, that wasn't working and after a few more names, Don quickly realized I wasn't going to respond to his verbal taunts. He came up the steps, solid heavy footsteps, and I broke out into a cold sweat.

Really? Couldn't he just go and make trouble somewhere else?

No, like a cat with a mouse, he'd found a new toy.

With his foot, Don kicked me in my butt and I almost lost my balance, but I managed to catch myself before I face-planted in the wet paint.

There was something really degrading about being on your hands and knees in front of someone who wants to kick the snot out of you. I just couldn't figure out how to get up so that I could at least try to face him. Before I could make my move, he planted his foot on my wrist.

"Come on, Don, I gotta job to do."

"Make me."

Right, I was a hundred pound weakling and I was supposed to make big, huge Don do something he didn't want to do. Pinching my lips together to keep any unwise remarks from erupting, I took my other hand, dipped it in the paint and continued painting. This time, I wasn't as careful as I had been and I got a few splashes of paint on the boot that held my left wrist captive against the porch.

Moving faster than a guy his size should be able to, Don jumped up with a roar and grabbed both my arms below the elbows and shoved them into the can of paint.

Something inside of me snapped.

I'd had enough.

I jerked out of his grasp, and grabbed onto his leg with one of my paint-covered hands and said, "Not another time, you son of a bitch!" I wasn't even worried that my mom would hear me use profanity.

I just couldn't stand it anymore.

I stood up as straight and as tall as I could and I glared up at him, paint still dripping from my hands. Surprised at my resistance, Don took a step back to get away from my paint-covered hands. Not willing to completely surrender, he sneered, "Go inside and tell your mommy you might get hurt."

"Get lost."

I couldn't believe I was standing up to one of my bullies!

I felt like I was ten feet tall.

Don continued to taunt me as I walked into the house, right over the nice, new paint job. I knew I'd have to fix it later, but there was no way I was going to get the job done with Don standing on the sidewalk. The familiar blanket of shame dropped over my shoulders as I headed for the kitchen to wash all the paint off my hands and arms. But as I scrubbed away the paint, I realized that I had finally stood up to one bully.

Now if I could just do it again at school tomorrow.

CHAPTER 9

The doorbell rang.

"Kevin, can you get it?" Mom's voice rang out from her bedroom.

I peeked out the window before I went to the door, as had been my habit for months now. The man had his back to me, but at least I knew it wasn't one of the neighborhood bullies.

"Uncle Henry?" I didn't know he was coming over. "Come on in."

Uncle Henry wiped his feet on the mat before he came into the house. "I see you're painting the back porch."

My eyes flew to his face.

What else had he seen?

That last thing I needed was for word to get out among the family that I was the butt of all neighborhood jokes.

"Yeah. I thought I'd help Mom out."

Uncle Henry nodded but didn't say anything. He just seemed to be waiting.

"You want to sit down or something?" I wasn't used to playing host. Dad had always done this, and if not Dad, then Mom. I felt strangely uncomfortable under Uncle Henry's steady gaze. "Can I get you a glass of water?"

Uncle Henry shook his head. "No, thanks. I'm fine. But I'll take a seat in here." He walked into the living room. I'd turned on the television as I usually did after a confrontation with one of my bullies.

Television was my safe escape.

I sat down on my toy box as Uncle Henry sat in Dad's chair. He looked good in it. Even though they weren't related, Uncle Henry and Dad shared a lot of the same features and it made me feel good just to be in the same room with him.

"So, Kevin...I was driving by just a little while ago and it looked like you and another boy were having a confrontation."

I didn't say anything.

I didn't dare breathe.

What was I to say?

I knew Mom had been keeping my problems a secret...in Irish Catholic families, you don't breathe a word of your problems to anyone.

Ever!

Uncle Henry seemed prepared to wait as long as it took. His eyes held mine, but they weren't threatening or mocking. They didn't reflect the fear and confusion I saw in Mom's eyes whenever I came in cursing or crying after I'd been attacked yet again.

"So, Kevin...what's going on with you?"

Nice.

An open-ended question.

The kind that requires a bit of thought.

What did he want me to say? This was making me feel like I was failing a pop quiz in history class.

After my silence stretched far beyond anything that might have been civil, Uncle Henry squared his shoulders and just came out with it. "I saw that kid push you around and then push your hands into the paint."

Well now, isn't that just great? Now my abject humiliation could just make the rounds of the family. Mom had managed to keep it quiet this long, but that couldn't last.

"Kevin, I think you need some help standing up to these kids."

My eyes popped open.

I hadn't expected understanding and compassion. Even though it was Uncle Henry. I'd expected to be told to stand up for myself. To "punch them in the nose" in my dad's words.

To my horror, my eyes filled with tears and I pushed them away with impatient hands. I let out a great sigh and said, "Dad said I should just punch them in the mouth."

Uncle Henry's lips twisted into a quirky grin, but he controlled that very quickly. "And most of the time I'd say he was right. What you're going through is the same thing a lot of boys go through. Growing up male is a pretty tough road. I had my share of being bullied."

What?

Uncle Henry bullied?

No way!

Uncle Henry smiled at my expression. "Yeah. I was the butt of every joke for miles until the summer between tenth and eleventh grade.

I shot up over a foot and I put on a lot of muscle mass because I was doing manual labor that summer. In eleventh grade, no one dared cross me."

Was it really that easy?

That simple?

But I was years away from being in eleventh grade. I wasn't sure I was even going to survive the coming school year.

"I didn't punch Don in the nose, but I did try to stand up for myself."

"I saw that, Kevin. I was real proud of you. If it had been me, I would probably have chucked the whole can of paint at him. But then, you would have had to explain to your mom why you needed more paint to finish the job."

We laughed together, and for one of the first times since Dad died, I felt an easy camaraderie with a male role model.

"Uncle Henry, how do I get these idiots to stop picking on me?"

There. I'd said it.

Out loud.

I'd asked for help.

Not that I hadn't been asking Mom for help. But, with Mom, it was so totally obvious she was out of her element I'd only used her as my shield by having lunch with her every day the past few weeks.

Uncle Henry pulled out a newspaper ad from his pocket. "I've been looking at this place. They teach things like karate...it's called a 'martial arts' studio. I just wondered if this might be a good thing for you to try." I looked at the black and white ad that Uncle Henry had in his hand. The figures reminded me of Big Jim with their muscles and poise as they stood on one foot and had the other foot kicked out as if defending themselves against a foe.

There was a flicker of something inside me.

This was exactly what I needed.

But I knew Mom couldn't afford the class fees. She could barely pay for our house and the food we ate. I wondered if I doubled my paper route, I might be able to manage the cost of the classes.

Uncle Henry interrupted my thoughts. "I never gave you a birthday present...no, the chain was your Auntie Dee's idea. I couldn't settle on something that was just right."

My hand reached up and grasped Dad's ring hanging on the end of the chain Auntie Dee had given me at the beginning of the summer.

"So, if you're interested," Uncle Henry paused and looked very intently at me, "in taking these classes, I would like to pay for them as my birthday gift to you. What do you say?"

What did I say?

Inside my head I said, HELL YES! Please teach me how to beat the crap out of the Don Blaylocks and Tony Capitanis of the world.

I wanted to beat the shit out of everyone who had ever hurt me, but I knew I couldn't say that to Uncle Henry, so I copied his manner and just nodded as if I were still considering his offer. "That might work for me."

"Well then, Kevin, let me know when you're ready." With that, Uncle Henry got up and headed for the front door.

"Wait! Don't you want to talk to Mom?" Uncle Henry had never come over just to talk to me.

In fact, he'd never come over without Aunt Dee.

Something was up.

"No, Kev. I came to talk to you. Let me know what you decide." And with that, Uncle Henry left and I was left wondering if I had just experienced a Cinderella moment with Uncle Henry as my fairy godfather.

I picked up the newspaper clipping he had left behind. As I read and re-read it, Mom came out of her bedroom. If I didn't know better, I'd say she had been in there listening the whole time to our conversation.

"Uncle Henry just offered to give me martial arts lessons as my late birthday present."

Uncle Henry and Aunt Dee

"That's nice." Mom pretended to be only vaguely interested, but now I could see how much she wanted this to work for me, to somehow protect me in a way she couldn't. "What did you say?"

"I told him I would think about it."

But really, I had nothing to think about.

I had nothing to lose.

※ ※ ※ ※ ※

Parlin Junior High was about a mile from my house, just down the street from Everett High. Again, I carefully chose my route, avoiding the projects on Cherry Street and keeping my distance from other neighborhood kids who walked in the same direction.

Every step I took, I wondered if I would feel different if I knew how to defend myself.

Okay, the real truth was that I wanted to learn how to beat up my tormentors.

Before I even got to school that first day, I had decided I was going to take the karate lessons.

Anything was better than this gut-wrenching fear I felt every time I left my house.

On my first day, school flew by.

I don't know if word got around I'd stood up to Don Blaylock or if everyone was too busy sorting out where their classes and lockers were that they didn't have time to mess with me, but I made it through the day unscathed.

I headed over to Mom's office because that was now my habit.

"What are you doing here, Kevin?" Mom looked surprised to see me.

"I figured I'd hang out here until it's time for you to go home."

Mom looked away from me, fiddling with some papers on her desk.

Her lack of response was odd. Finally she spoke, "Kevin, I don't think it's such a good idea anymore. You're thirteen now and it's time for you to stand up on your own two feet."

What?

She was yanking away my one safe place?

Talk about throwing me to the wolves.

"Kevin, it's not like that." Mom could always read my face these days. "It's just that it doesn't look good, you coming over here to avoid spending time with your friends."

"They're not my friends anymore."

"I'm sure once you work things out, you'll be friends again."

I turned away from her in disgust. She was cutting me loose. It was now just me against the world. I left her office and stormed home, anger in every step.

I'd cooled off by the time I got home.

I'd made my decision.

I called Uncle Henry. "I want to do it."

"Great, I'll come right over and pick you up. We'll get you enrolled today."

Within fifteen minutes Uncle Henry picked me up and we headed over to United Studios in Everett Square. Funny thing, it was just a few doors down from Gino's Pizza. I was still smarting from Mom's refusal to let me hide out at her office until it was time for her to come home, but deep down I knew she was doing the right thing.

I really did need to figure out how to stand up for myself, but the thought terrified me.

I was nervous clear down to my toes.

What if I couldn't do this either?

I was rotten at sports and everyone knew it.

What if the karate instructors took one look at me and just started laughing?

When we walked up to the doors of the studio, a big part of me wanted to chicken out, but I hid those feelings from Uncle Henry. I didn't want him thinking I was a total wimp.

Paul Taylor met us, and, I immediately liked him. He wasn't one of those teachers who sizes you up and finds you wanting. Instead, he looked at me and said, "So, you want to learn karate?"

Of course I did.

Why else was I here?

But as a kid, you pretty much don't say anything to an adult that might make him think I was a smart-aleck.

To save time and any misunderstandings, I just nodded my head.

"Great. Let's go over the things you'll need to get started." Paul and Uncle Henry went over the options and we decided that I would begin a class once a week on Wednesdays. Two days away. I'd need a uniform, a white gi and a white belt. I knew a little something about belts in karate. Big Jim was a black belt, and I knew that was my goal, but I decided not to say anything to Paul yet.

Once all the paperwork had been signed and Uncle Henry and I walked out of the karate studio, I began to have my usual doubts.

What if I couldn't do it?

What if I failed, as usual?

Maybe Uncle Henry was just wasting my time and his money.

Yet, every time I started to bring up my doubts to Uncle Henry, he managed to divert me and before the afternoon was over, I had a brand-new gi, I'd been signed up for classes, and Uncle Henry had a look on his face like a kid at Christmas. "Well Kevin, I think you're about ready to start on a new phase of your life!"

He could say that again.

New phase indeed.

To learn karate meant I might actually have some kind of a fighting chance to finally stand up for myself. I'd no longer have to be the butt of everyone's jokes. Maybe I wouldn't be the last one chosen for a game. For the first time in a long time, I began to feel optimistic that there might be an answer for my inability to blend in with the crowd.

For Tony it was sports.

As for me, maybe, just maybe, it was karate.

※　※　※　※　※

I couldn't believe it.

I stared at my brand new white gi, the white belt, and the canvas bag Uncle Henry bought for me to carry my gear in. I could hardly wait for Wednesday.

My classes were held immediately after school on Wednesdays. That Wednesday, instead of trying to get Mom to let me hang around for a couple hours, I went directly to the karate studio.

The entrance was your typical double glass doors, looking like any commercial shop in the area. It was when you entered that the environment changed.

The foyer was designed for peace.

I was to bow when I entered, which indicated I was leaving all my outside cares out where they belonged. I made a quick requisite nod of my head, did a quick change in the locker room, and arrived at the mat ready for class.

Paul Taylor, my sensei, or instructor, was a powerful looking man with a black gi and a corresponding black belt. If I hadn't met him when Uncle Henry had signed me up, I would have been horribly intimidated. But, because I'd sensed a peace and a sense of kindness in him, I came to my first class a little cautious, but determined to do my best.

Paul's method of teaching was designed to give every student the opportunity to succeed. If I made a mistake, he didn't give me an impatient glare.

Instead, he would calmly say, "Try again, Kevin."

I couldn't believe that it was truly that simple, but his gentle encouragement made me want to try even harder to do well. By the end of class I was worn out, but elated. To my friends, I probably still sucked at sports, but to me, I had found a teacher and an environment where it didn't hurt to make mistakes. This time, when I left, I bowed with a little more attention to the idea of leaving what occurred on the mat, "on the mat" and leaving what was in my outside life, "outside."

What I couldn't do, however, was forget how much I enjoyed my first class. That night when I went to sleep, for the first time since Dad died, I had something to smile about before I closed my eyes.

From that point on, my entire life was structured around my Wednesday karate class.

I wasn't as aware of people teasing or bullying me unless they actually punched me or knocked me down.

I suspect that my lack of fear took a little of the fun out of it for my tormentors.

They had to step things up in order to get my goat.

I'd managed to save enough from my paper route to buy myself a Barracuda jacket. It cost me $45 bucks, and Mom was happy I had come up with the money because she just couldn't squeeze that much out of our budget. I wore that jacket to school with great pride. I felt like I fit in a little better because everyone who was anyone was wearing a similar jacket.

Tommy Mason decided that I was walking around the school just a little too carefree for his comfort. In my world you were a bully, a bully's right-hand man or one of the bullied. Tommy, because he was a really big kid, fit the bully bill pretty well. His horrible temper sealed the deal. When Tommy got mad he would turn so red you would think his head would pop, but this was accompanied by such a terrifying, crazy rage, it really wasn't funny.

I no longer had my Barracuda jacket, but my friend still had his.

One day in shop class I was wearing my Barracuda jacket and happened to catch Tommy looking at me. Quickly, I averted my eyes, but I wasn't fast enough.

"Whaddya looking at? Huh?" A chill went down my spine.

I just knew he was gunning for me.

Thinking that he couldn't possibly do anything in class, I kept my back to him and continued working on my project. The rapt attention of everyone around me on their particular projects told me that Tommy had come over to our table. I wanted to shudder, but couldn't show weakness.

He punched my shoulder from behind, knocking the paintbrush out of my hand and I saw, to my dismay, that some of the paint had gotten on my new jacket. I still refused to turn around and face Tommy. The truth was, I was absolutely terrified. Our shop teacher had stepped out of the room and absolutely no one was going to come to my aid.

Before I could anticipate his intentions, Tommy grabbed my can of paint and upended it all over my jacket. "Are you going to do something? Huh, Loser?" He taunted me to the sound of muffled laughter from all the other uneasy boys in the room. They were all just glad he hadn't chosen to pick on them. Of course I wasn't going to do anything. Tommy was a wall of human flesh. I was a good foot and a half shorter than he was.

No, I couldn't do anything but seethe deep down inside. I grabbed towels and kept the worst of the paint off the floor, but my jacket was ruined. The anger that was born after my father died was beginning to affect me like a cancer. I seethed with impotent rage. I wasn't going to cry, not in front of him, but I just wanted to turn on him and beat the crap out of him.

What had started as a small ember deep inside was beginning to grow. I was actually afraid of the white-hot lava-like anger that I knew could result from all this internalized rage. For a moment, I went back to my old thoughts that I had no purpose in this world other than being a punching bag for bullies like Tommy. This had been going on for so long, it just seemed normal, and, yet, I knew it wasn't right.

The snickers stopped when Mr. Carver re-entered the room, but the bell rang right after so he never knew why there was a spattering of paint on the floor by my workstation in shop class. He never asked either.

That night I went to sleep with a new goal.

I was going to become so good at karate that no one would ever bully me again.

I had murder in my heart that night, and, I believed that learning martial arts would be my weapon.

※ ※ ※ ※ ※

At my next karate class, I entered, bowed, and prepared for class with great determination. That's when I noticed Tony. He came through the double doors without bowing, he was already wearing a white gi and white belt, and in case I made any mistake about his purpose for being there, he came right up beside me, gave me a punch on the shoulder and said, "Hi, Kev."

My stomach clenched in on itself.

This could not be happening.

This was my outlet, my secret weapon, my way out of a life of torment.

I was perilously close to tears when Paul Taylor entered the room, and I'd been to enough classes that I knew the routine. I returned his bow and readied myself for class.

I don't know if Paul knew my history with Tony or not, but, magically, he seemed to sense that having Tony right next to me would be my undoing. He had Tony change places with another boy so that he was out of my line of vision. Again, once class started, I had only eyes and thoughts for the instruction. I wobbled a few times with a new kick or pose and I'm pretty sure I heard Tony's snicker, but I managed to stay focused on what I needed to do to get the look of approval I so dearly needed from my instructor.

As Paul taught us the moves, kicks, and blocks, he also taught us the principles of karate, about honoring ourselves and others. I really wanted to believe that everything he was saying about learning the key principles of karate would shape me into the best version of myself.

Within the first few weeks, I had learned if I put both my physical and mental effort into my practice, I would improve.

Today, Paul focused on other aspects of the philosophy of karate.

"Here you will learn the code of karate etiquette. However, you will not leave what you learn here; you will carry it with you and honor its principles at home, school, and work."

I sure wanted to know if Tony was listening, but I didn't dare look at him; Paul was still talking. "You must have control over your impulses at all times, this means you will practice self-control in all aspects of your life. This means you must focus on any task at hand and make sure you finish what you begin."

Paul's words seemed to be designed specifically for me.

When I saw Tony enter the dojo, I wanted to quit immediately.

But, looking at the fire in Paul's eyes, and seeing the passion he had for his love of teaching karate reinforced my determination to finish what I started.

I would learn karate.

※　※　※　※　※

October blesses Everett with a blaze of gold, orange, and red, and this year was no exception. I'd stopped visiting my dad on a daily basis.

I just didn't have enough time.

But, I made sure to stop by for a chat at least once a week.

Today I was on my way to St. Therese's for catechism class. I'd left early so I could stop by the cemetery on my way to church. I got down on my knees and brushed away the fallen leaves from Dad's gravestone. There were no flowers there today and part of me wished I'd thought to bring some, but looking overhead at the colorful canopy of trees, I realized God had given Dad a far more colorful bouquet than I could have.

My conversation with Dad that day was more about what I was learning in karate. It made me proud to tell Dad I'd advanced to the point where I was now able to spar with other people in my class. As a beginner, I had learned basic stances, balance, blocks, kicks, and straight punches done as a kata or a series of karate techniques done in a specific order. Once I advanced, I was able to actually begin sparring with my classmates and this, for me, was really exciting.

This past week I had managed to block my opponent's kicks and punches exactly as I'd been taught, and then with what I still think was a lucky break, I'd managed to knock him down. In the spirit of our dojo, I immediately gave him a hand up and then we bowed at one another to indicate mutual respect.

I didn't speak out loud much at Dad's grave site anymore. I'd begun to just have conversations with him in my head no matter where I was. Maybe that was why my visits to the cemetery had become less frequent. I was really glad I hadn't been talking out loud as I heard familiar voices coming my way.

Tony.

Dave Braden.

And Don Blaylock.

My favorite trio.

Tony spotted me first. "Hey Kevin! What's your dad got to say today?"

Jerk, I thought.

I quickly got to my feet and turned to face them, saying nothing. They were heading to St. Therese's too. We were all in the same confirmation class together. There were days I really wished I could move to a different neighborhood, but that simply wasn't my reality. We'd lived on Dartmouth Street for a very long time and Mom was not in a position to move anywhere else. I was trapped with my neighborhood tormentors until I graduated high school. I felt the familiar buzz of anxiety and anger inside of me.

These three weren't here to be friendly today.

Somedays they actually behaved pretty well, but Tony had been kicked out of the karate studio for misbehaving.

He had bullied one of the younger students and Paul Taylor immediately booted him out the door.

I'd been there that day and witnessed Tony's humiliating ejection from the dojo. I'd been very, very happy that day, but I don't think I let it show on my face. Today, however, I could tell by the look on Tony's face that he was still smarting and intended to take it out on me.

Without even realizing it, I took a well-balanced karate stance designed to protect myself from attack. When Tony came at me with a kick, I deflected it, and with a swift turn of my hand, twisted his foot, then swiped his other leg out with a quick move of my leg and he fell to the grass with a thud. He scattered dried leaves in his haste to get up.

I didn't like the look in his eyes, and if he'd come at me again, I think I would have been pounded within an inch of my life.

Something on my own face must have gotten through to him because instead of relaunching an attack, he turned to Dave and Don and said, "Come on, let's get going."

I watched the trio walk toward the church leaving me in a daze.

"Well what do you know, Dad? It worked!"

I followed Tony and the other two boys to church where we sat for an hour in utter boredom in desks designed for much smaller bodies than ours.

The entire time, I wasn't listening to Father Walsh at all. I was marveling that I'd finally bested one of my bullies and had lived to talk about it.

I could hardly control the grin on my face.

CHAPTER 10

For the entire weekend, I felt better than I'd felt in a very long time. Dad's advice, "Just punch them in the nose," was sounding better and better. I'd managed to best Tony and he hadn't done anything yet in retribution. I ate better and slept better than I had in the past six months.

The next school day saw me once again trampled and pummeled.

My triumph hadn't lasted very long at all.

Mr. Lewellen's algebra class was on the second floor of the junior high school, and I had just gotten to the top of the stairs when both Don and Dave suddenly appeared and surprised me with Tony behind them. They let out an ugly roar of laughter as they grabbed my books, notebooks and tossed them all the way down the stairs. As I turned around and lunged to try and save my homework, one of them gave me a great shove and I fell down thirteen stairs, feeling every single one of them with various parts of my body.

The physical pain fell into the category of something I knew how to handle. It was the taunting, the laughter, and ridicule that hurt much more.

I've been told all my life, "Sticks and stones may break my bones, but names will never hurt me."

That's crap.

The taunting hurts worse.

Whoever came up with that saying has never been humiliated by the entire student body of their school. Everyone just stood where they were until I opened my eyes.

Great.

Since I wasn't dead or bleeding, they all just returned to what they were doing as I lay there on the landing, papers all around me until the bell rang, the doors above me slammed shut and I was enveloped in a dusty silence. Gingerly, I rolled to one side and pushed myself up. I'd be black and blue by tomorrow, but there didn't seem to be any really serious injury.

What I couldn't believe is that absolutely no one had come to my aid. Not one single person asked if I was okay. No one protested when my books and papers had been tossed into the stairwell. My triumph over Tony had been very short-lived, and, maybe even a stupid move on my part.

Now he knows he can't best me using karate so he's taken to using a couple of big goons to do his dirty work. Don and Dave were both significantly bigger than most of the kids in my class, and they scared me. I was still one of the scrawniest guys in school and definitely no match for them.

I knew I should have picked up my books and papers and be marked tardy for class, but I just couldn't face the jeers, smirks, and whispers I knew were waiting for me in Algebra class.

For the first time in my life, I left school early and without permission.

Mom worked as a secretary for the truant officer, so this was kind of a big deal for me. If I got picked up for skipping school, it could look bad for her, but today I just didn't care. It was only one class. It's not like I'd be reported for skipping school for last period.

I walked home as slowly as I possibly could.

This was one time when I didn't feel I had to check around every corner before taking any particular route because I knew my three biggest tormentors were safely tucked away with Mr. Lewellen. It was probably the freest forty-five minutes I'd spent. I didn't exactly go home right away. I just wandered, hanging out here and there until school let out and the streets became noisy with kids walking home from school.

From my protected spot behind a tree, I saw Tim Cross heading home. If there was anyone who was smaller than I was and picked on even more than I was, it was Tim. I really don't know what happened to me, but it's like something inside of me just snapped.

And I did something I'm not proud of.

As he came alongside the tree, I jumped out at him and laughed when he dropped his books.

It felt good, this sense of power I had over the other "last pick" of the neighborhood. In the back of my mind, though, I knew what I was doing was wrong, but that didn't stop me from taking a stance, and then shooting my foot out in a front kick toward his stomach. He folded in half, exactly as I'd expected. What I didn't expect was him grabbing my ankles from his position on the ground and wiping me out. I put my elbow into his spine, by now he was really giving me a fight. I don't know how, but he managed to move in such a way that my elbow popped and his elbow connected with my eye. There had been no yelling or shouting. Our entire skirmish had been accomplished with soft grunts and growls. Tim backed away from me, picked up his books and then ran away.

Touching my tender eye, I knew I would end up with a shiner.

OK, idiot! What was that all about? You're not supposed to pick on other people. He's another you!

How stupid could I be?

I couldn't imagine what Paul Taylor would say if he ever found out I had used my few weeks of karate training to beat up another kid.

I felt lower than dirt.

That moment, I realized I had to control my temper, which is something Paul really stressed during our classes. This was going to be one of my most difficult tasks because even now, as sore and bruised as I was, my temper was still red hot.

When I got into the house, I started punching the wall in the hallway. One hit, then another, and another. I kept it up until my knuckles were raw and bleeding.

I felt a little better, but it was going to be a little hard to explain to my mom why there were dents in the wallboard.

※　※　※　※　※

The next karate session, I walked into the dojo with a new sense of humility.

I felt like I should tell Paul what I'd done, but there was never a moment when I could do it. So instead, that room with the panel walls and red carpet became my sanctuary. I knuckled down and did everything Paul told me to do. I learned from him that if I failed at something it wasn't a failure. He'd just look at me and say, "OK, now try it again."

And I would.

I would do it again and again, and again.

It didn't matter if it was a stance, a kick, a punch, a block. I would do my moves over and over until I had them absolutely perfect. For the first time in my life, I felt like I had some kind of control over my body. I earned my orange belt pretty quickly, and I was pleased with my success, but that wasn't enough.

I wanted more.

Each belt progression required more knowledge, more abilities, with the pinions, kicks, punches, and blocks increasing in difficulty.

Paul explained exactly how to do something, "Lift your leg like you're lifting it over a bicycle, then snap and spin out."

That was a difficult kick for me, but with Paul's continued encouragement, the training became so ingrained I could almost do this move and the resulting katas in my sleep.

Before too much time had passed, I was taking karate three days a week and getting progressively better. I also became better at incorporating discipline, honor, self-control, and character in my life. I had nothing when I started at the karate studio except a burning desire to learn.

I got a couple of things out of learning martial arts.

The first was self-esteem.

I finally felt good about myself.

The second was making friends.

Tommy Spellman was one of my new friends at the dojo. He was a little younger than I, but he had been taking karate for a couple of years already. Instead of rubbing it in my face that he knew more than I did, he just encouraged me, and showed me in slow-motion how to do certain moves so I was more graceful in my transitions. He was always sick with massive allergies, but that never stopped him from training. He'd cough and sneeze and keep right on training. His example inspired me to train even when I didn't particularly feel like it.

Another friend I made was Bobby Carbone, who I learned to call Chooch because he would frequently wear a train engineer hat. He was a green-belt when I started at the dojo and he, too, took me under his wing. They both showed me what to do and what not to do.

For the first time in my life I was in a place where I wasn't judged and found wanting.

It was really different for me.

In the dojo, we were taught to bring other students up and along and to never make fun of someone else.

As I'd seen with Tony, behavior like that earned immediate expulsion from the studio.

At the dojo, I learned there were places in this world where people weren't there to make you feel bad. They were there to make you feel good. While it wasn't a team sport, it was a team effort in bringing everyone along.

We were all individuals.

As individuals, we helped one another get better.

At the dojo, my emotional maturity began to develop.

※　※　※　※　※

By Thanksgiving, I'd found something to be thankful for and was eager to share it with Aunt Dee and Uncle Henry. We often went to their house for Thanksgiving, so for the first major holiday after Dad's death, being with them made it more bearable than if we'd just stayed at home.

Aunt Dee cooks as well as some great chefs I know and walking into her home to the smell of turkey, onions and sage with the spicy undertone of sweet potatoes and pumpkin pie, made me feel embraced by the aromas. Mom and Jeanne, arms loaded with food, headed right for the kitchen, but I went into the living room where Uncle Henry was turning on the television to get ready for the first football game of the day.

"Hey Kevin," he hugged me and gestured for me to sit down with him. We hadn't talked much since he'd taken me to the dojo to sign up for my first karate lessons. "How is the karate going for you?"

Where did I start?

I'm sure my big grin gave him the answer he was looking for, but I needed to let him know just what a difference it had made in my life. "It's great. I'm already an orange belt, and I'll be tested for my yellow belt before Christmas."

Uncle Henry didn't know anything about karate, but he listened and smiled at my obvious enthusiasm. We talked for a bit about what I was learning and I could tell he liked hearing that I was making new friends at the dojo.

"And how are things going with these other kids who have been pestering you." He didn't come right out and call them bullies, but we both knew who he was talking about.

"They're still around. I did manage to knock one of them down when they kind of ambushed me one day." I wasn't going to tell him that my victory was very short-lived or that I'd tried to use my karate knowledge to pick on another worm of a kid in our neighborhood. I still burned with shame over that event and I knew I would never do that again.

"Keep at it, Kevin. The thing you need to remember is that you won't always be around those bozos. Unfortunately, you're stuck with them while you're going to school, but after that, college will really open your eyes to all the opportunities there are in the world."

Uncle Henry's words really stuck with me.

I hadn't really thought that once I was out of school, my world could possibly be different. But just entering into the world of martial arts, I began to see that there were possibilities I'd never known about before. On the days when things seemed to be their worst, I kept telling

Thanksgiving with Uncle Henry and Aunt Dee kept us going.

myself that one day I'd meet people who didn't care if I couldn't play baseball or if I was always picked last for any team I'd ever been on.

We all shed a few tears that Thanksgiving Day, each of us missing Dad in our own unique way, but for the first time since the funeral, I realized whether I liked it or not, life was moving on and I had to make something out of it. I could certainly go on missing Dad, but I also had to make a life for myself and learning karate had come along just when I was searching for something to fill the emptiness that had defined my life since his death.

After dinner, Uncle Henry and I retired to the living room to snooze and watch football while we listened to the chatter of female voices coming from the kitchen with its amazing smells still emanating from the room. Aunt Dee always made a turkey soup from the carcass of the bird, and I knew she had already started cooking it as they cleaned up from dinner. We would feast on leftovers tomorrow and then, Saturday, come back over for that amazing soup.

Sometimes traditions are the greatest gifts in life.

▓ ▓ ▓ ▓ ▓

Shortly after Thanksgiving, Mom asked, "What do you want for Christmas, Kevin?" I hadn't really given it much thought. We'd gotten through Thanksgiving without Dad pretty well, but I was really dreading Christmas without Dad.

"I dunno."

I could tell Mom had something she wanted to talk to me about, and talking about Christmas presents was just her way of getting the conversation started. She waited patiently for me to speak, but I really had no ideas.

"Do you want to tell me what those dents in the hallway are about?"

Of course she would see them.

How could she not?

"I punched the wall because I was mad."

Mom nodded. "You know we're going to have to fix those, don't you?"

"Yeah, Mom." The truth was I'd taken to punching the walls when I came home to vent my ever-simmering anger. It took less and less to set me off any more. I'd actually punched a hole in the wall of my room the other day. Maybe Mom had seen that one.

When I was at the dojo, I'd have a go at the great huge bag hanging in the corner. I was so scrawny that my punches and kicks didn't even move that behemoth, but I'd watch some of the older black belts come in and practice on the bag, and their kicks and punches certainly moved that bag.

That's what I wanted to be able to do.

It should have been no surprise to me that Mom gave me a canvas bag. I knew it was an expensive gift for her to give me, but she probably figured it was less costly than repairing the walls of her house.

The side effect from this gift was I overcame another fear I had always held.

Being in the basement.

As long as I can remember, I'd always been uncomfortable down in the basement of our house, but we had no other place in the house where we could set up my new canvas punching bag. It wasn't quite as massive as the heavy bag in the dojo, but it was a good start for me.

We cleared an area in the basement and with Uncle Henry's help, we hung my punching bag in one corner of my space and for the first time in my life, I felt like I had a space of my own. It wasn't much to look at; it was your typical cellar, dark and dank, with only one little window high up on the wall. But, for my purposes, it provided privacy and a place to work out even when I wasn't at the dojo. I wasn't totally dedicated to karate yet, but I knew I liked the feeling of competence it gave me. It was something I could do and feel good about myself.

My basement studio became my haven.

I still had some dark and dangerous thoughts and feelings, especially if I'd been picked on at school. But now, instead of coming home and destroying Mom's house, I would head directly to the basement and punch on that punching bag until I was literally bending it in half. I'd do this for almost an hour every evening because I had that much anger built up inside of me.

Even if I'd worked out at the dojo, my anger kept me company.

I would compartmentalize it while I was in my karate classes because I was in a safe environment and always learning something new. But once I got home, my emotions would spill out and having no other outlet, I'd punch my punching bag until I finally exhausted my quota of anger for the day.

I didn't really talk to anyone about my anger.

It was just as difficult to describe to Mom and Uncle Henry or any of my teachers as it was to tell anyone that I was being bullied.

I felt, somehow, there was something wrong with me.

That I was deficient in some way.

I didn't see other people walking around with this constant anger in their hearts, but I suspect I was able to hide it pretty well myself. No one ever really knew I was angry until I let loose on something like a wall or a punching bag.

When dad died, I had determined that anger was better than sadness, so I was probably coping with my grief by allowing anger to come to the surface rather than sadness. The last thing I needed was for one of my tormentors to see me crying because I missed my dad. Life was tough enough already; I didn't need people to know I was a weakling and a sissy on top of it all.

⬛ ⬛ ⬛ ⬛ ⬛

The rest of the school year zoomed by with the only a couple of truly remarkable events. The first was being called into my counselor's office one day. "Kevin," he was looking at a paper on his desk rather

I was 16.5, a black belt, and ready to meet girls

than looking at me, "it's come to my attention that Tommy Mason has been bothering you."

Why couldn't he just say it for what it was?

He was bullying me.

But I just kept my mouth shut. For all I'd been through, I knew it was a whole lot worse if word got out that I ratted anyone out.

My silence made him look up at me. "I know you've been taking karate lessons. Why don't you just show him you know how to defend yourself now?"

Me?

Defend myself against a wall of a kid like Tommy Mason?

My counselor must live in a different world than I did.

He was expecting an answer and all I could do was shake my head. I didn't know the answer to that. Sure, I was taking karate and I'd managed to get Tony off my back, but after trying to beat up the other "last pick" of the neighborhood and being bested by him, I hadn't tried my karate techniques on anyone outside the dojo.

No help there.

He just wanted me to be able to beat up the kid and his problem would be solved.

I figured my success over Tony had just been a fluke and while it kept him from bothering me, it hadn't prevented him from gathering the forces and getting other people to mess with me. They were even going so far as to throw things at Mom's car and the house at night. Mom would just clean it up, her lips tight with disapproval, but she knew there was nothing we could do to stop them unless they were caught.

They knew that I knew and that was enough for them.

Karate was great for my self-esteem, but it hadn't totally taken care of my bullying problem. I had no answer for my counselor and his question stayed with me for a long time.

Then, right at the end of the year in homeroom, Tommy Mason and Don Blaylock got into a fight. Our teacher had stepped out of the room and I'm not quite sure what set it off. I was just glad I wasn't the one on the receiving end of the punches. Tommy looked like an onion with his white hair and his roly-poly body, wide in the middle and tapered at the top. Everyone in the class could see he was worked up because his face was so red, it was almost purple. Don was about the same size as Tommy, so it was finally like he was picking on someone his own size. It was over in a matter of minutes, but Don beat the crap out of Tommy. After I got over being afraid he'd go after me next, I actually felt good that someone had taken care of Tommy.

I had my blue belt by this time, and, I still didn't feel like I could have taken Tommy in a fight. Interestingly enough, after Don beat him up in front of my entire homeroom, he just stopped bullying people. For the last few weeks of school, I continued to give Tommy wide berth, but like a beaten dog, I gradually felt confident walking past him without worrying whether he would knock my books out of my hand or get me in a choke hold until I gurgled.

The summer I turned fourteen, I learned a lot of things.

I discovered weight lifting.

A new friend.

Girls.

And alcohol.

CHAPTER 11

My fourteenth birthday came and went and wasn't nearly as difficult as it had been last year. Last year, I was still in the midst of such overwhelming grief that to celebrate anything as trivial as my birthday was just not on the agenda. This year, I was invited to "go out" with one of my new friends, Lionel, someone who didn't know my past history of being bullied.

Lionel just seemed to like and accept me for who I was.

This was an unusual experience for me.

As a result, I was very grateful for Lionel's friendship. When he invited me to go out that Saturday night for my birthday, I was more than happy to accept.

Lionel seemed to know everyone and was a big kid who was very comfortable in his own skin. I think that's what first made me notice him, his genuine ease with whoever he was with. The other thing that was great about having Lionel as a friend was he lived miles away from my neighborhood, effectively expanding my world fourfold.

For me, this was huge.

By going over to Lionel's house and spending time there, I became familiar with him, his family, and his neighborhood. I'd found a safe haven, away from my home neighborhood on Dartmouth Street, which continued to represent daily warfare for me.

I headed over to Lionel's house early in the afternoon.

It was a warm day toward the middle of June, and I felt incredibly carefree and happy that day. Once I'd left my neighborhood where I'd carefully checked down each street before walking into the open street, I dropped my vigilance and just enjoyed being a fourteen-year-old kid on a summer afternoon.

Lionel's mom opened the door to my knock. "Come on in, Kevin."

She was so used to Lionel having a lot of friends, she never seemed to notice I was the only white kid for several blocks around. Like Lionel, she just accepted people as the person they showed up as. If I were a jerk, I'm sure I'd hear about it from Mrs. Beane. But, because I'd been raised to be respectful and say, "Yes, ma'am," or "no ma'am." Mrs. Beane accepted me and afforded me absolute respect as well.

I found Lionel in his bedroom, where he was reading magazines. His bedroom was as messy as mine, so I picked up a pile of clothes from the chair by his desk and after looking for a better place to put them, just set them on the floor, but neatly so I didn't make a bigger mess.

"What are we going to do today?" Lionel asked me.

I shrugged. I was hoping he'd have some ideas.

"OK, I have some ideas. There are a couple of girls who want to meet up with us a little later if you don't mind."

Mind?

Was he kidding?

I was barely able to hold my head up among most of my friends much less look at a girl with any hope of getting her interested. After losing Patty to Tony last year following Dad's death, I'd sort of sworn off girls.

But that sure didn't keep me from looking at them and wishing they would just see me as something other than a scrawny kid who got beat up all the time. And if Lionel said he knew some girls, you could count on them being the best-looking girls around.

I could hardly wait.

After a brief word with his mom, we headed out to just hang out.

This could mean any number of things, and at first we just walked over to get something to eat. Lionel wanted Chinese food, so we ate at a late afternoon Chinese buffet at an all-you-can-eat place, something guys like us really appreciated. It wasn't something I ate very often, but I found I really liked sweet and sour chicken and could hardly get enough of it.

Afterward, our stomachs contentedly full, we headed over near the park where Lionel usually hung out. Just about the same time we arrived, three gorgeous girls appeared.

"Lionel!"

"Hey Baby!" He hung his arm over the shoulders of the tallest, and threw kisses to the other two who smiled coyly at Lionel. They threw sidelong looks at me as if to say, "Who's this?"

Lionel casually said, "Kevin's celebrating his birthday with us tonight," which was met with squeals of delight.

I'd never been the object of such obvious excitement from the opposite sex except when my mom and sister wanted me to do something for them that I didn't want to do.

This was different.

It felt a little like adulation or something.

That sure wasn't a feeling I got every day!

Just then, Lionel spotted someone approaching from the other side of the street. "Hang on ladies, we can finish intros later, what are you drinking tonight?"

Drinking?

I was cool with this.

I'd had a beer or two when I stayed at my cousin's house, and while I knew underage drinking was frowned upon, it was still done all the time.

The girls all wanted Tango, which I discovered later to be a blend of cheap orange juice and even cheaper vodka. As soon as they told Lionel what they wanted, he loped over to the man approaching the liquor store, which just happened to be right by the park where we were hanging out.

Convenient.

Lionel really knew how to pick them.

I watched as Lionel talked briefly with the man and then handed him a wad of bills. I wasn't sure how this worked, but it looked to me like Lionel had just talked someone into buying us some booze.

He came back with a big grin and said, "Let's get this party started!"

Two of the girls grabbed one of his arms and giggled with delight. The other girl, not to be undone, came over and grabbed my arm and I was suddenly one of the group. I'm still not sure how it happened, but for that one night it was as if the "kick me" sign I had worn so long on my back was missing. I was hanging out with friends, some of the girls, and I really, really liked how it felt to have a girl hanging on my arm.

Just a couple minutes later, the man came out of the liquor store and quickly glanced behind him to make sure the clerk didn't watch him hand a case of beer and a bunch of bottles of Tango off to a group of kids. Yet, this is exactly what he did. He even handed Lionel a couple of bucks saying, "You gave me too much money."

Wow, an honest guy. Lionel waved it away, saying, "No man, you did us a big favor. See, it's Kevin's birthday and you just helped us get this party going in style. We appreciate it."

As I said, I knew that underage drinking was not a good thing, but alcohol itself didn't seem to be a problem. Dad and my uncles always had alcohol at the house, sometimes having a couple of beers every night, and definitely drinking a whole lot more than that on weekends and whenever we got together for family celebrations.

It made perfect sense to me to celebrate my birthday by drinking.

We headed to a more secluded corner of the park. At this point, Lionel and one of the girls, I think her name was Wendy, headed back to the store and came back with a bunch of junk food; chips, pretzels, and a bag of donut-like things I'd never had before, but tasted great until I started drinking beer.

The girls seemed to like the way the donuts tasted with their Tango.

We munched, drank, talked, and laughed for what seemed like hours. After I'd had several beers and was laughing about how the world seemed a little tilted, the girl who had become my "date" for the evening coaxed me into drinking a little bit of her Tango. I tried it, and, for the sake of continuing the party mood, I proclaimed it to be the nectar of the gods.

Lionel couldn't have me be the only one joining the girls so he took a slug or two of the Tango. I noticed he went back to the beer, but, at this point, I was totally past caring. I was having fun, more fun than I'd had for a very long time. At no point did I think about how much I missed my dad or how horrible I felt my life was. Tonight I was riding high on the ecstasy of being with fun people and having a good time without anyone getting hurt.

We climbed the slide numerous times, eventually turning it into a train where we alternated girl, boy, girl, boy, girl and tried to get down the slide as a unit. It never worked, but we sure laughed at our efforts. The girls got on the swings where Lionel and I pushed them so high, they screamed in terror, which only made Lionel grin and then we pushed them even higher.

The merry-go-round was probably a mistake, as one-by-one, the girls stumbled off into the trees only to return looking pale and a little shaky, but unwilling to be the first one to call it an evening. As for me, I felt invincible.

I drank more beer.

Then, I drank more Tango.

I didn't need the snacks. I liked how I felt after downing each drink.

Then things got a little fuzzy for me. At one point, I remember we stumbled down the street toward Lionel's house, still laughing inanely at anything we said. I couldn't even tell you when the girls finally took off for their own homes, and it was just Lionel and me, but I do recall lying on the ground and Lionel pulling at my arm and saying, "Come on, Kevin. This is a street man. You can't sleep here!"

I tried to help him help me up, but all I could do was giggle and roll. I think this is finally how he got me out of the street. The next thing I remember was Lionel encouraging me to climb into a grocery cart. It was impossibly high and it kept moving, and no matter what I did, I couldn't quite negotiate the task. Finally, Lionel just picked me up and dumped me quite unceremoniously into the cart and started pushing me.

"You want to bunk at my house tonight?"

"No. Mom ud be wurringed." I meant to say she'd be worried but I had lost control over the movements of my tongue, teeth, and lips. I knew exactly what I wanted to say, but my brain wasn't communicating with my mouth at all. My stomach was beginning to feel distinctly unwell and all I wanted to do was close my eyes and sleep, but every time I closed my eyes, I got impossibly dizzy. It didn't help that Lionel was pushing me home over the sidewalks of Everett, which are not known for being even. They canted and caved, depending on how old the trees were that grew beside the sidewalk. The ride home jerked and jolted me so badly that I wanted to get out and just lie down in the cool grass.

But Lionel was having none of that.

He grunted and heaved as he pushed me up the final hill toward Dartmouth Street and when we got to my house we had to reverse the process to get me out of the shopping cart. Finally Lionel just upended the cart and I got my wish, I was finally lying on the cool grass right next to my front steps where I began to heave my guts out.

With the perfect time of a mother, Mom opened the front door. Lionel squinted in the sudden glare of the light, grinned his wide grin and said, "Good evening Mrs. Kearns."

"Good evening, Lionel. What's wrong with Kevin?" She started to come down the steps.

I could hear in her voice I was going to get into some major trouble if I didn't think fast, and that's something I've learned to do quite well over the years. "Don't worry, Mom. We had Chinese food for dinner. I think I might have food poisoning."

That's all I had to say.

It's all I could say as my stomach revolted again and I was unable to speak for several minutes. Over my retching, though, I could hear Lionel expound on my symptoms of eating Chinese food.

"Why aren't you sick, then, Lionel?"

She didn't believe us. I could tell.

"Kevin ate like a huge bowl of that sweet and sour shi-er-stuff. I can't stand that stuff myself. It must have been that."

I could feel Mom's hand rubbing my back. Even if she suspected that I had been drinking, she probably couldn't stand to see me so miserable. "Kevin? Do you think you can come inside yet?"

Between Mom and Lionel, they got me inside and once I got on my bed, I passed out. I'm not sure what else Mom and Lionel said to one another that night because I was completely unconscious. Mom checked on me early the next morning and I could feel her fury from the doorway because I was no better. In fact my head was pounding and I thought the weight of an elephant was sitting on it.

It was Sunday and Mom had to deliver my papers, complete with the extra heavy advertising section inserts.

By early afternoon, I managed to drag myself out of my room and into the kitchen where my sister took one look at me and said, "Chinese, huh? Not likely." Then she went back to her teen magazine and ignored me as I made myself a piece of toast.

Nothing else sounded good.

To make things better with Mom, I went out and mowed the grass, swept the sidewalk like Dad would, washed her car, even polishing her rims until I could see my face in them.

Nothing was ever said about my Chinese food poisoning.

Mom ignored that just as she had ignored my being bullied.

※　※　※　※　※

That summer I turned fourteen, I also got turned onto another hobby.

Weight lifting.

I always felt that I looked like a hundred-pound weakling.

At the dojo, I met a guy named Keith who invited me over to his gym do some weight lifting. Keith was a major body builder, and I wasn't really sure if I wanted to be as crazy as he was with his powders and carb loading or protein packing and whatever else he did.

What I did want were the muscles that Keith had.

Because I'd known him at the dojo for almost a year, I trusted him. At the dojo, he followed the rules of bringing others along with you and when I asked him how he got to be so muscular, he grinned at me and said, "You gotta pump iron!"

When he offered to teach me how to get into weight lifting, I was more than ready. I worked out with him two days a week, spent another two days a week at the karate studio and then Friday and Saturday nights with Lionel and his friends drinking and carousing. It was a great summer. I managed to avoid Tony, Dan, and Dave for just about the entire summer. Every once in a while, I would cross paths with one or the other at the beach or pool, When they weren't together as a trio, I discovered they left me pretty much alone, but to be on the safe side, I avoided them whenever possible.

I knew delivering papers wasn't going to afford me the lifestyle I was looking for as a high school student.

I started looking around for other jobs.

My first dishwashing job was at the Silver Fox.

My supervisor was a senior and a total bully. I lasted there a week and then I left. It was enough I was bullied at school, I wasn't going to stand there and be bullied at work too. Due to Mom's connections, I found a job as a dishwasher at my favorite restaurant. I used to really like their food until I saw how big they grew their cockroaches, but I continued working there because it paid more than delivering papers. Despite the fact I developed eczema on my hands and arms from always being wet with dishwater, I stuck with it. One of the guys who worked there told me to never go down to the basement alone because there was a roach down there cutting up a roast beef.

On Sundays, I helped my Uncle Freddy at the flea market. He worked as a contractor there and wanted me to learn how to sell. "Kev, you're going to be my front man here," he'd tell me as he showed me how to sell the small items. It was anything and everything he could find. He had garages all over town and would collect all kinds of junk, clean it up and then sell it.

You name it, he sold it.

Shoes, nails, ax handles.

One time, he had so many ax handles, he had me charge only a dollar to get rid of them. I learned to sell like a pro at those flea market events.

The plan behind all this frantic industriousness was to buy myself my own weight set, which I did. That way my basement studio now contained my punching bag, a new leather one because I'd already split the canvas one Mom had gotten me at Christmas, a chair, a table, a lamp, and my new weight set. At first, I didn't really notice anything, but as time went by every time I looked at myself in the mirror, I noticed I had muscles. They were pretty small at first, but they were there.

I never thought about the fact that drinking and training for both body building and karate were not exactly compatible.

Everyone I knew drank, from my parents and relatives to the neighbors.

It's just what everyone did.

I just liked the goofy feeling it gave me. After my first big night with Lionel, I learned to moderate how much I drank so I wasn't falling down drunk ever again. I became as good a negotiator at the alcohol stores as Lionel was. I credit learning to be a salesman at Uncle Freddy's flea market sales for that.

I would see guys come to the liquor store from the gym where I worked out. "Hey Vinnie, can you do me a favor, can you get me a case of ponies?" We'd get the beer or whatever we were drinking that night, run down the street to the schoolyard and make sure we were enough out of sight that we didn't get caught.

To a certain degree, I knew drinking was wrong, but I didn't equate it with poor health the way I did with cigarettes. I was offered pot, and tried it once, but it was so much like smoking that I just didn't get into it. I learned to drink the most disgusting beer in the world, but because they were cheap and had a higher than average alcohol content, they seemed like a pretty good deal to us. Three of those and I'd be singing in the trees.

The interesting thing about drinking was that from time to time, I 'd actually hang out with Tony, Don, and Dave because the alcohol numbed my feelings toward them, and they liked how easy I could get alcohol. Derek, my former model-building friend, would often be with them and he would turn into a mean drunk when he drank. I learned really quickly to avoid him if he came around when we were drinking.

One night, Lionel came over to my house, and, as we walked down the street, we could hear the sounds of loud voices and raucous laughter.

"You know these guys?" Lionel asked me.

"Yeah."

It was hard to explain to him my relationship with Tony, and, even harder to justify thinking about spending time with Don and Dave. How do you tell your best friend you still desperately want these guys to be your friend after they have humiliated and tormented you for years?

Being in high school was opening my eyes to new options and opportunities, but this was still my home neighborhood. I felt some kind of loyalty to the idea that because we were "neighbors" of sorts, we should also be friends.

Every Sunday, I'd sit and listen in church to the gentle teachings of Christ to "love your neighbor" and "turn the other cheek." Each time I heard them, I'd be filled with a sense of hope that perhaps the next time they pestered me, I would rise above it and then finally things would be better and we could resume the friendship I remembered from my childhood.

"So, do we join them or find our own party?"

Lionel was willing to do whatever I wanted.

With him at my side, I figured it was safe enough to join Tony's party tonight so we rounded the house to the yard where the party was in progress. It was evident that no parents were around because it was quite a big party and a lot of alcohol was being passed around.

Lionel grabbed a beer and no one said a word. But when I reached into the bin to grab a beer, Derek grabbed my wrist, twisting it cruelly and said,. "Who said you could join us?" His beer-laced breath testified to his state of inebriation and I decided to just back off."

"Sorry. Just wanted to have a little fun."

Derek threw my wrist away in a gesture of disgust. "This here is a private party and you've crashed it." His eyes narrowed and his fists clenched. Derek was the closest thing I'd ever seen to a mean drunk and I recognized our mistake immediately.

I threw a look at Lionel.

He watched quietly.

I'd never seen him come unglued and attack anyone, so I really wasn't sure what to expect from his corner.

"I guess we'll leave then." I backed away and put some distance between myself and Derek. Despite my training and weight lifting activities, he still outweighed me by at least forty pounds, so I wasn't interested in a physical confrontation.

Derek advanced as I continued to retreat, still backing up. I wasn't going to turn my back on him. Taunts and jeers joined Derek's protest, and I knew that while Lionel might have been able to stay at the party, my presence wouldn't be tolerated that night.

"Hey man, hold this for me." Lionel had moved quickly to Derek's side and handed him two bottles of beer. Derek's meaty fists closed around the bottles and while I knew they could quickly be turned into weapons, his brain wasn't functioning fast enough to process that information.

In the same moment, Lionel spun me around and we turn and ran from Tony's backyard. Once we reached a dark space between the

Lionel was wise beyond his words: "You need new friends."

streetlights, he tugged my arm again and without speaking we both rushed into the dark yard on our left and backed into a bush. There were no lights on in the yard so we were virtually invisible. I could hear our harsh breathing and I was sure that at least Lionel could hear my heart pounding. We stayed there and listened as we heard a couple of pursuers running past the house out by the street. A few shouts and then retreating footsteps told us that they weren't all that interested in catching us.

Once it was quiet again Lionel turned to me and said, "Man, if those are your friends, you need some new friends."

He was right.

I'd spent so much time trying to repair my friendships that I'd lost sight of the most important thing.

They were no longer my friends.

Regardless of the issues they might be facing at home, perhaps they were abused in a variety of ways, it was time to stop excusing and justifying their behavior.

They would never be my friends again.

While that realization made me feel as if I'd lost something, I felt a strange sense of release.

●　●　●　●　●

Because of the void it filled in my life, I continued working at the dojo and each time I progressed to the next belt, I'd bring home my certificate, plaster it on the wall in my basement studio, and stare at my certificates as I worked out. Here was solid proof, evidence, that I wasn't a worthless piece of crap.

But why did I still feel like that?

At the dojo, I would go into a kind of Zen zone and my thoughts never really bothered me much, but when I was working out in my dark basement studio, a lot of the old thoughts, taunts, and memories of being bullied would float around the room and haunt me.

I'd work out for hours down there.

Punching the punching bag.

Kicking and punching the cement block walls to toughen myself up.

I just knew there was sure to be a pretty ugly and bloody showdown at some point.

It dawned on me one day as I was training that I was preparing for the fight of my life.

Sure, I was learning martial arts and how to do the punches, kicks, and kata drills I needed to learn in order to move up in my belt ranking. But what I focused on when I was in my studio basement was my hatred of the boys who had once been my friends before turning into my biggest tormentors.

It didn't take much to re-ignite my anger.

I could spend one Saturday night drinking with the guys in the neighborhood and think that everything was cool between us only to get up the next morning to find someone had printed in white shoe polish on Mom's car ugly words and phrases. One Sunday, I caught her out there washing it off before I woke up and realized she had probably been doing it a whole lot more frequently than I had known.

That was enough to send me down to the basement for the rest of the day to punch, kick, and pump iron until I was absolutely exhausted.

It was really difficult for me to reconcile what I was learning at the dojo about discipline, honor, character, and self-control when my real life was still so miserable. And yet, I knew that without karate, I would have had no way out of my life, and I would have been completely without hope.

So, I continued to work on my karate.

Once I reached my purple belt, I was able to get the black gi. Somehow putting on a black gi made a difference in how I saw myself. It was a huge badge of honor to wear a black uniform, and at this point, I was able to learn to use weapons.

Weapons.

I really liked the sound of that.

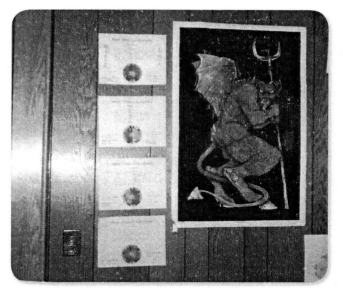

I posted my certificates on the wall.

Using weapons would come in really hand when I finally had the confrontation I knew was coming. It was no longer just a possibility. The only way I was going to finally get my core group of bullies off my back was in an OK Corral style confrontation.

I was basically preparing for a fight to the death.

I know that's not something easy to hear from a teenage boy, but that's where I was in my life. It didn't matter what I did, how much I tried to find a peaceful way to end the battle between me and my bullies, it was ultimately going to come down to a stand-off battle between myself and them.

At the dojo, I had learned how to blow out a candle with the speed of my hand. There would be a lit candle on the table and I would stand in front of the candle with bent knees, like I was riding a horse. I would snap a punch at the candle in an attempt to blow it out with the speed of my punch.

The first couple of times, the flame barely wavered, but I'd watch Paul snap his punch and when it was my turn again, I tried to do it exactly as he did. Then, when I went home, I made sure I had candles and matches and took them into my basement studio. Over time, I developed my own training for this exercise where I would have a bunch of candles lined up. As I improved and my speed increased, I would be able to knock out the flames on more than one candle at one time.

My hands got so fast you often couldn't even see them.

Pretty soon, the entire focus of my life became training. I started private lessons and small group lessons at the dojo to get more individualized training, and also began training there three, sometimes four days a week.

I worked for my black belt harder than anyone.

Before I knew it, I had reached my brown belt and I was preparing for my black belt test.

In three short years, I'd gone from being the last pick in everything to getting ready for my black belt.

▦ ▦ ▦ ▦ ▦

The day of my black belt testing dawned.

I was almost sick to my stomach with anxiety.

Mom made my traditional "testing day" breakfast of blueberry pancakes, but I could hardly eat even though I knew I had to have enough energy to face the day-long series of grueling tests. Ever since Christmas, all my gifts had been Kung Fu magazines, karate magazines and all types of karate weapons . I had spent every moment out of school focusing on this day.

I pulled out my clean, black gi.

We were warned to wear black today because after six to eight hours of testing, our white gi would turn black. Once the testing began I realized the physical aspects of the black belt assessment were much easier than the mental ones. By the last hour, I was so exhausted mentally and physically I just wanted to throw up.

Finally my last battle.

There, in front of the Grand Master in his big chair, I had to spar with another competitor and I was paired with a wimpy looking kid with pasty white skin. This sparring session was an all-out fifteen minutes, no holds barred.

Hours spent in the basement, were hours I spent developing my own self.

At first I was a little disappointed that I'd been paired with such a weakling, but this was my first but not last experience where looks can be deceiving.

He gave me a really decent fight.

We were given marks on technique, prowess, how well we accomplished our movements, and, finally the fight. I've never been more focused in my life than for those fifteen minutes.

All those hours spent in my basement, punching the punching bag and hitting and kicking the cement walls came to my aid that day. While in my basement, I'd visualized kicking or punching either Don, Tony or Dave. The human body gives when you assault it. The cement wall doesn't. If I hit or kick my opponent as hard as I hit and kicked that wall, there would be no stopping me.

As I sparred, though, I didn't have murderous thoughts in my mind like I did when I was practicing in my basement. My thoughts centered on the disciplines I'd been taught over the past several years. That's the training that sat on my shoulders as I fought and I performed well.

I was sixteen years old and I'd just passed my black belt test.

I was on top of the world.

The huge diploma I was awarded made me puff up with pride.

I had finally done it.

And I'll admit, I wanted more than anything to shove it in the faces of all the kids who had beaten me up.

But as time passed, I thought less and less about my former friends and more and more about my future and the people I wanted in it.

Why had I spent so much time and energy with a bunch of losers and posers?

Until Lionel pointed out that I could chose different friends, I hadn't even realized I had a choice in the matter.

CHAPTER 12

"Ma, can I use the car tonight?" I poured my bowl of cereal for breakfast, and added milk until the flakes were dangerously close to spilling over onto the table.

Mom looked up from the morning paper spread out over the kitchen table, her eyes slightly unfocused until she adjusted her glasses to look at me. "Why do you need the car?" She pushed the sugar container over to me.

I sighed.

Every time.

Mom, my sister Jeanne, and me

Every single time, it had to be a battle.

"It's my birthday, Ma. Lionel and I are going to the beach."

"But Kevin, I thought we'd have pizza and then have Uncle Henry and Aunt Dee over for birthday cake." Her eyes showed her hurt. I knew she wouldn't put up too much of a fight, but even this was more than I wanted to deal with today.

"I'm sixteen, Ma. I'm too old to be taken out for pizza and blowing out candles on some crummy birthday cake." I didn't want to hurt her. Since Dad's death, Mom had become just a shadow of the person she used to be, and it seemed that just about everything I did managed to hurt her somehow. I pushed the container of sugar back to the center of the table.

No more sugary milk for me.

I was now a man.

"No birthday cake?"

If I hadn't seen it about a hundred times now, I would have thought she was going to cry. I wasn't a kid any more. I relented, just a little. "How about brownies instead? Would that be OK?"

Immediately, the lines of worry between her eyebrows eased and she smiled at me. "That would be nice."

"But let's plan it for tomorrow, OK? I want to spend my birthday at the beach with my friends tonight."

"Sure, Kevin. If that's what you want."

"So I can have the car?"

Mom nodded and turned back to her newspaper and cup of coffee.

I love it when a plan comes together.

I wolfed down my cereal, dropped the bowl into the sink, and headed down to the basement for my morning workout. Birthday or not, I had a workout schedule that I stuck to seven days a week. I was more disciplined about this attention to my body building and karate training than anything else in my life.

Except for, maybe, girls.

Even though I had big plans for later in the day, the minute I set foot in my workout space, time stopped. There was no rushing what I had on my schedule.

Upper body.

Lower body.

Kata.

While I didn't want my mother to fawn over me with birthday cake and pizza, I did have a plan for blowing out candles. Still one of my favorite moves, extinguishing candles with the speed of a punch from either hand, I had already determined that I would privately blow out sixteen candles at the end of my practice.

I could easily extinguish two candles at once, and was getting really good at three.

Today I wanted to try four at a time. I lit four tapers and lined them up in a row. Staring at the yellow flames, the four individual flames blended into one as I tilted my head from side to side, evaluating the best path to use.

With speed that impressed my karate instructor, Paul, I made my first punch. All four flames disappeared leaving four smoking wicks. As the four lines of white smoke drifted upward, I made a wish.

I wish Dad could see me now.

Gone was the lost and lonely boy I had been when Dad died.

I still missed him, but had finally figured out I was probably going to carry that empty painful hole in my heart for the rest of my life. There was no getting around it, I was always going to miss him. Only when I was alone did I allow myself to miss my dad. Down here, in the darkness of the basement, I could be sad, and even cry if I wanted to.

But I didn't want to cry today. I straightened, picked up the lighter and lit the four tapers again.

POW!

Four lines of white smoke rose toward the ceiling.

Another wish.

I wish my life had a point.

Aside from weight training and karate, I just wasn't sure what I was going to do with myself. I was getting through high school okay, but I was really just scraping by.

What was I going to do with my life after that?

Another four flames beckoned. Another carefully considered and executed punch. Another four lines of smoke moving upward. This time, I felt a sense of satisfaction and confidence. Maybe my life already had a purpose. I was finally doing something I was really, really good at. Four years ago, I never thought I'd be punching out flames with the speed of my punches.

I wish Mom would come out of her funk.

That wish surprised me.

I had been noticing more and more how lost she seemed. Right after Dad died, she really crumpled emotionally, but she had to pull things together. She was a single mom with two kids to raise, and she'd done the best she could. I'm not sure if she would ever fully understand me. She and my sister were a lot closer than I was with her. But, I did care about her, and as I made that wish, I knew I really did want her to find a way to live and enjoy life again.

I guess both of us had to just get past our grief and move on. Not that the neighborhood bullying had helped matters any. The past year had been worse on my mom than on me. Countless times, I'd come home to find the yard and fence covered with toilet paper or the car egged or painted with shoe polish in garish and ugly phrases. Several times, I'd caught her cleaning things up before I got home, and, it had taken me a while to figure out it was her one way of protecting me.

It turns out, the eggs and shoe polish were just the starting point. One day I came home to find the windows on the car had been bashed in. It was as if they were saying, "We can do anything we want to you at anytime. There is nothing you can do about it."

She couldn't stop the bullying, but she did what she could to prevent them from hurting me by hiding the evidence before I could see it. I love that she tried so hard.

But she couldn't stop them.

It seemed no one could.

The final four candles. One blow. Out!

I wish I never had to see my tormenters ever again.

Right.

Like that was going to happen.

"Kevin!" Mom's voice sounded at the top of the stairs. "I smell smoke!"

I laughed as I made sure the candles were completely out. "It's just me, Ma, blowing out my birthday candles."

⁂

That summer I was going out with several girls at the same time and my social schedule had gotten pretty complicated. Who would have guessed I would ever have such a problem? When Lionel suggested we go to Revere Beach for the evening, we decided it would simplify things if it would just be the two of us.

We'd go to the beach and see who was there.

Beaches are built for red-blooded American boys because they are heavily populated with gorgeous bikini-clad girls pretending they're

My bullies decided to escalate their threats

only there to work on their tan, even though through their eyelashes they watch us guys wander up and down the boardwalk.

It was a great game of pretense, each side ignoring the other.

Yet, everyone knew it was part of the game.

As I'd learned when I first met Lionel, he seemed to attract the most lively, beautiful girls around, and, before we'd been at the beach very long, we found ourselves escorting a group of bathing beauties who modestly covered their bathing suits with a sarong-like cloth, which exposed one beautifully tanned thigh all the way up, hiding just enough of everything else to be tantalizing.

I breathed in a huge breath of moist, salty air and thought, "I like having a birthday."

Yes. Celebrating my birthday wasn't the burden it had been for the past four years.

That evening with the lights of the Ferris-wheel glowing behind me, I looked out over the water and realized I'd come a long way in the past few years. I'd gone from being a lost, little boy who didn't know how to face the world without his dad to a karate black belt surrounded by people who enjoyed being with him and didn't have any intention of hurting him.

If anyone had told me I'd be this happy by the time I was sixteen, I would have called them a liar. Even in my most fantastic dreams, it never occurred to me I could ever be happy again.

※　※　※　※　※

Just as my contended thoughts filtered through my consciousness, I felt a savage kick at the base of my spine that sent me staggering into the sand off the boardwalk. I heard the gasps of the girls and then heard the familiar, ugly, mocking laughter.

Laughter that haunted my thoughts, and my dreams both day and night.

The crumbs I had dubbed the tiresome trio.

Don, Tony, and Dave.

They stood there guffawing as if they'd never seen anything so funny. I didn't have to look over my shoulder to see it, I'd seen it often enough over the years to know what they looked like.

The rage that boiled up inside of me was raw and vicious.

For all my good intentions, the fight I'd been preparing for but had secretly hoped would never be, was upon me.

It had always been bad enough when they'd bullied and humiliated me in school in front of kids who had witnessed the same scene, day in and day out.

But tonight, of all nights, on my birthday?

No.

I refused to tolerate this.

My life had moved on, past these bozos.

Now, here they were, pulling me back into my old life, the one where I was a victim, a punching bag, the object of ridicule, shame, and torment.

I was no longer their willing punching bag, in my mind I had moved on to something better than their sick and twisted inner circle.

Their laughter and taunts grew louder, attracting a crowd.

Just as they had intended, public humiliation was their forte and they had certainly mastered it. There was nothing more public than the boardwalk on a summer evening: families shouting with glee from the top of the Ferris wheel, and couples wandering hand-in-hand, seeking romance in the dusky moonlight.

Idiots.

Their idea of fun was perverted.

I had moved on to a different life, but just as it is with most insecure people, they didn't like me changing their world. They couldn't stand the idea I might decide I no longer wanted to be their willing punching bag, and that I had stop wanting to be readmitted into their sick and twisted inner circle.

They didn't like me, but no one else could have me either it seemed.

As in the scene of *The Last Samurai*, time seemed to stand still.

I could hear each grain of sand fall to the cool and damp surface of the beach. The sounds of laughter and music faded into the background.

I breathed in an out, feeling the breath reach deep inside of me, all the way down. My heartbeat, first incredibly fast, slowed.

Thrub, thrub, thrub. I heard it in my ears.

With very deliberate movements, I pushed myself up, and, with my back to the laughing trio, I considered how I would take on this situation.

Lionel came up by my side and said, "Bro, you need some help? I can get you covered."

And he would, too.

But this was my fight.

Still looking out over the ocean, my back to my enemy, I shook my head. "No, thanks. I got this." He looked at me for a long moment and then he gave me a single nod and backed away. I never asked him what he saw in my eyes at that moment, but I know it was dangerous. He quietly got the girls back, and a loose circle seemed to form around us.

As I dusted off the damp sand from my pants and shirt, I planned my approach.

I had the angel in the form of Paul Taylor on one shoulder. "Remember, Kevin, only use force in self-defense."

I knew this.

I had trained myself to become a killing machine.

For the past three years, I'd been practicing how I would destroy Dave. Every single kick in my basement had his name on it. Each time I'd punched my punching bag, it had been Tony's nose, and every other blow that knocked out the flame of my candles had been to Don's gut.

On my other shoulder was the devil, that deep-seated molten hatred that wanted revenge. I could taste it, the salty, bitter dish I'd been looking for.

Again, Paul Taylor's voice echoed in my head. "Remember Kevin, don't use your skills in malice."

Was it malice to protect myself?

Was it malice to defend myself?

Was it malice to wipe the sneering smiles off their faces for all the pain they had put me and my mother through over the years?

Yeah, it probably was.

But I didn't care.

This was my fight, and I knew how to win, even with the odds of three to one.

In that moment, I was a psychopath. I didn't care what happened to me, I just knew I wanted to hurt these guys, snap their necks.

The first move was to break Don's knee. It opened, bringing him down forward, and with a rising ridge hand, a strike to the throat. People get their jaws broken with that move to the Adam's apple. You can forget it. He's never swallowing again.

A heel stomp to the back of the leg. A Judo chop to the back of the head. Knife hand right to the back of the neck would snap his spine.

Eight seconds tops.

I punched Tony straight in his handsome Italian face, the one his mother loved so much She never saw what a piece of shit her son had become. Stomp the knee from the side and he basically wouldn't walk right for the rest of his life.

Do I?

Don't I?

It kept going back and forth.

There was no pain or agony in my decision. It was just a matter of choosing.

Do I choose to go against my moral code and destroy this SOB or do I walk away?

"Effing wimp." Dave just couldn't help himself. "You're nothing but a pansy." Years of being abused at the hands of his mother, father, and older brother had turned Dave into such an ugly human being that if he'd been a dog, he would have been put down.

My response was a blank, cold stare.

From the moment I got up from the sand, I hadn't moved. Everything had played in my head like a movie, but my body and my face revealed nothing.

I brought my hands to my side and slowly assumed a boxing stance: left leg forward, right leg back, ready to go.

Combat ready.

Weight on my back leg, my strong leg.

My hands weren't raised.

I was inviting an attack.

Hands raised above the waist was considered assault. I knew the law.

It was like waving a steak in front of a lion.

"That's the best you can do? Kick me from behind? Now who's the effing wimp?" I challenged.

I didn't blink.

Didn't swallow.

My breathing was so controlled and relaxed that it didn't even feel as though I was breathing.

I had rehearsed this scene so many times in my head, I knew exactly what I was going to do and I wasn't worried about myself.

Me as a senior in high school

I knew I was going to come out of this just fine.

If they choose to engage, at least one person was going to be dead, and it wasn't going to be me.

All their bullshit. All the time I had spent training. All the hours I hid and skulked down alleyways to avoid these jokers.

Everything that had happened between us over the years all boiled down to these thirty seconds.

It felt like a year.

But it was over in half a minute.

My intensity was like touching the surface of the sun. I could feel it burning inside of me, aware of the desire over the years, and, yet, I was completely at peace.

These three bullies didn't deserve to walk the planet. They weren't human beings.

They were bugs and I wanted them to give me a reason to squash them. I hated these three people more than I have hated anything in my entire life. Without the training I'd learned, the self-control I'd been trained with, the core beliefs of character, self-control, etiquette, and honor, I would have killed three boys that night.

Self-control came to my rescue.

I'd been taught I could use lethal force only in self-defense. Being kicked from behind was not a threat to my mortal being, even though it had ignited justifiable emotions erupting from the past years.

I'd come right to the very brink of hell and my training had taught me exactly how to take out these three. But, the difference between me and the people who bullied me all my life, is that I knew the difference.

Somewhere down inside of me there was a glimmer of compassion.

It's true, if I'd taken these three guys out, most people wouldn't blame me. It was well known throughout the Everett school system that I had been systematically bullied for many years.

But I knew that just because I was angry, I had no right to take their lives.

The true distinction between being bullied and becoming a bully myself was knowing the difference between self-defense or aggression.

There were two warriors inside of me battling for control.

One side was the angry warrior, the one who wanted to effing kill them for all the crap they had put my family through: my father dying, my mother being tormented with worries and burdens beyond bearing. The other warrior, the trained one, realized these idiots, while culpable, weren't really at fault.

Deep down, I knew they were assholes, idiots, morons, losers. They were living a life they hated, and the only way they felt better was when they made someone else around them feel worse. For years, I'd been that scapegoat.

No more.

I don't know how far I would have taken that moment on the beach if they'd chosen to pursue it. But Tony, the one I'd known the longest, watched me closely after I'd said, "Make a move."

He was looking for a sign of weakness, a lack of resolve. This sign would indicate he could then strike, and if he could, he would.

But he didn't see that opening. He saw the level of anger I was controlling. He knew that I wanted to and was willing to kill him and his two henchmen tonight.

I'd spent the better part of three years training and getting stronger to have the fight of my life dissipate as if nothing ever happened.

In the blink of an eye, it was over.

Lionel watched everything unfold. The girls just knew there were a couple uncertain moments with a few ruffians who ultimately decided not to mess with us.

In the blink of an eye, Tony and company turned tail and retreated.

Relaxing, my hands and feet left their boxing stance.

Not a single punch had been thrown.

I put my arm over the shoulders of the pretty blonde next to me and around the waist of the freckled red-head who was as Irish as I was. The rest of the evening, we laughed, talked, and acted like the teenagers we were.

As I drove Lionel home in Mom's ugly, peach-colored Maverick, a 1977 with no power steering and 55-AC, I relived my earlier happiness. Our evening at the beach could have turned very, very ugly. Fortunately, I discovered that most bullies are cowards.

When they know they're beaten, they will retreat.

Lionel had been pretty quiet most of the way home. He finally broke the silence. "What happened back there?"

What did happen back there?

"I think I discovered that anger isn't any better than sadness." That sadness from my father's death that I'd chosen to channel into anger had done nothing to serve me well in terms of my mental health.

I could very easily lost control there on the beach, and, instead of Lionel and me heading home as carefree as we'd begun the evening, I could have ended up in jail on murder charges.

Because it would have been murder.

They hadn't attacked me to the point where I feared for my life. They were looking to insult and humiliate me as they had done for years.

What I had learned is that by mastering karate to the point of becoming a black belt, I had something to fall back on. But it's not much different than learning to shoot a gun.

Do you fire the gun just because you have it and you can?

Or do you fire the gun because you fear for your life?

My black belt has taught me how to defend myself to the point of taking my opponent out, meaning I could have killed up to three people.

The difference is I chose not to.

* * * * *

The summer I turned sixteen stands out as one of the happiest of my life.

School was out.

I'd just earned my black belt in karate, and had achieved what had seemed like an impossible goal when I first started out on my martial arts journey.

Lionel helped me understand that my so-called friends wouldn't change.

So I made new friends.

I didn't want to be friends with a bunch of bullies and losers.

They were trapped in a way of life, a way of thinking, that meant nothing to me.

Earning my black belt taught me I could do anything I wanted. I just had to put time and effort into it.

Learning that my mom didn't have all the answers was another interesting revelation. When I was younger and would turn to her in tears, all she could do was console me and try to divert my attention from the immediate situation. Then she would give me the tired old phrase, "Tomorrow's another day, maybe you'll find that you're friends again." She was almost always wrong when she said that, but when I was younger, I had nothing else to cling to, so I earnestly wanted it to be true.

The shattered mirror I'd faced the day of my father's funeral seems to have been put back together. All the cracks are still there; there is no way of fixing the pain and hurt of our past. But the mirror, whole again, reflects who we become as a result of how we handle our pains and our newly discovered strengths.

"Hey, Dad." My voice floated on the early morning breeze. "You would have been proud of me last night." I stood beside Dad's grave, having placed a bouquet of flowers on it. "I finally got it, Dad. You said to 'punch them in the nose' and I pretty much kicked their asses without landing a single punch."

I sat down in the soft, cool grass, picking at a single blade, elbows on my knees. "You knew, didn't you, that I had to make my own way? It wouldn't have worked if you'd fought my battles for me."

Dad's easy ability to make friends wherever he went was the one thing I really envied. "I figured something out, too. The world's bigger than I thought it was, and there are people out there I actually like hanging out with. I have friends now."

The early morning, gray light moved away from the approaching rosy fingers of the sun.

I got up to leave and then turned back around.

There was one more thing I needed to tell Dad.

"I want you to know that you don't have to worry about me anymore. I can take care of myself now. It's funny, but I'm the guy I can count on now."

It was true.

Lionel and me today. Good friends will stand by you forever.

I was my own hero.

Dad knew I had to have the internal strength to stand up to my bullies, whether I did it physically or not.

At last night's showdown, I'd broken through a lot of barriers I'd been putting up over the years. My martial arts training had given me the physical skills I needed for the confrontation.

But, it was the belief I had in myself that was my real power.

That belief will be with me for the rest of my life.

EPILOGUE

In the intervening years between high school and writing this book, I became an entrepreneur. Imagine the faces of my bullies if they ever discovered I not only became a martial arts expert, but I began training others to do the same. I ran a gym called The Fitness Connection from 1995 to 2005.

In 2005 I sold The Fitness Connection to develop a new business, Burn with Kearns. You'd almost never believe what life had in store for me, a kid who had been bullied most of his life.

You gotta love the irony of life.

I had always been a fan of Ultimate Fighting Championship (UFC) and Mixed Martial Arts (MMA), and, when the reality TV show "The Ultimate Fighter Tough Season" aired in Beantown, I was there training with my old hometown friend and UFC striking coach Mark D. Kru (Kru meaning teacher). Mark was a rising star for coaches in the UFC and one of the fighters training with him at his gym was an up and coming UFC star.

In 2006, his rising star (we'll call him Casey for the sake privacy) had racked up enough wins to get him a shot at the light-weight title for UFC. At the time we met, Casey already had a strength coach from out of town, who he was very loyal to, and I admired his loyalty. But Casey was intrigued by what he was hearing about me...that I was "the guy to work with" in town.

His big title fight was fast approaching in November 2006. About three weeks before his title fight, his manager called me in a bit of a panic. "Hey, Kevin, Casey's hurt his back…and I mean bad!" You don't often hear panic in a manager's voice, but I heard it that day.

"He's what, three weeks away from his fight?"

"I know! Can you work with him on his flexibility?"

I'm a big fan of "when opportunity knocks" and in helping out someone in need. I agreed immediately.

This was a huge opportunity for me and I took it.

Casey's main coach was his brother, and as anyone in these circles knows, working with another coach can be tough going, but I knew I was up to it.

I went to Vegas on my own dime, and made the mistake of listening to someone say, "Sure, that hotel's just a coupla blocks away."

Fortunately, I'm an early riser and I'm determined. I looked at the 40 minute walk as an opportunity to plan out my strategy for the day's training ahead.

Our first day together was a bit rocky. Casey was tight, and Kru Mark and his team had worked together for a long time and viewed me, the outsider, with a little bit of suspicion. But, I knew my stuff.

I was there to do a job and it took every ounce of focus on my part to ignore the unspoken doubts of every other man on the team. They didn't know what I could do, and to them everything I did seemed wrong.

Shutting everything out but my main client, I focused completely on Casey and what he needed to do in order to get ready for the fight.

The day of the fight, they didn't call me over until three hours before the fight. I had no fingernails by then, but I was determined to have Casey in top condition.

About an hour before the fight, the tension in the room was so thick, it really could have been sliced with a knife. No one spoke a word. Doing nothing for that hour drained us.

But once we stepped into the corridor and the camera crew followed us into the ring, filming every step of the way, I knew I was a part of something huge.

I could hardly wait to phone home and tell my wife about this moment, but knew it would have to wait until the fight was over.

In the elevator, Kru Mark knew exactly how to lighten the mood so when we arrived at our level, the mood was much better. But this didn't satisfy Casey's strength coach who was really worried.

"He's too relaxed, man. He's too relaxed." His words hissed around me, and for a moment I accepted his fear. Then I remembered something I'd learned many years before.

"You can't control anything but your own thoughts."

His thoughts might be getting the better of him, but they didn't have to get the better of me. I was still focused on my fighter.

Only a few members of the team had badges that allowed them to stay in the room with Casey. I wished him luck and with his other trainers, we went to our seats.

It was all up to Casey now.

I'd done everything I could to help him win this fight.

But…that wasn't Casey's day. He lost a ton of blood in the fight because of a cut from an elbow shot, and he lost the fight on a decision.

I went home from the fight, having texted Casey, thanking him for the opportunity to have joined him in Vegas for his big comeback fight.

About a month later, I got a call. "Kev, it's Casey. I need to make a change in my strength training and I want to talk to you about it."

In December 2006, I took over Casey's strength training and went to work with purpose on Casey's weak back. Every day we trained, I thought how odd it was that the guy who had always been picked last, who had been bullied most of his school life, had now been chosen to be the guy to train UFC fighters.

It's pretty ironic when you think about it.

We worked every day in preparation for his next fight in April. While his fight in November had been tough, this fight was against the top opponent

In order to position Casey to win, we had to cement his mindset to be that of a winner.

"Do you like Tom Brady and Tiger Woods?"

"Yes."

"Are they pros?"

"Sure they are."

"Are YOU a pro?"

This question surprised Casey, but after a moment he firmly said, "Yes, I am."

"Then ACT like one!" I shot back at him.

At first Casey didn't know what to say.

"I DO act like one."

"No, Casey, you don't. You horse around during your off season, so that it takes tons of effort to get back into shape in time for a fight. From now on, there IS no OFF season! Got it?" I didn't get the name Dr. Evil for nothing. "If you want to be a pro, you do the work before, during, and after the event."

Almost as if a light bulb went off in his head, Casey turned to me and said, "I get it, Kev. No off season."

No off season became our mantra for the next three years we worked together.

Our next problem was the issue of Casey's back. I've seen way too many fighters who believe they have a physical disability that prevents them from rising to the top. In Casey's case, it was his back.

One day, just prior to training, Casey's manager called and said, "Kev, Casey's gonna bail on his workout today…says his back is acting up."

Forewarned is forearmed. When Casey called to cancel our workout, I played dumb. "What's up, bro?"

"Oh, my back's kind of tight. I think I'll just rest it for today and see how I feel tomorrow."

I let a moment of silence make him uncomfortable before I blasted him. "What, you going to play video games all day? Get over here and do your workout!"

It wasn't until I got off the phone that I realized arguing with a UFC fighter might not have been the smartest move of my career.

When he arrived, he was visibly unhappy to be there.

"Casey, I'm not sure how many people actually care about you and whether you do your best, but I do! We can work around your injury."

That might have been the first time he had ever considered a future without back pain. With evident optimism and enthusiasm, he buckled down and worked out that day.

There is NO off season!

And our next mantra: "When you change the way you look at things, the look of things change."

I got this statement from Wayne Dyer, and he's right. If you think you have an injury for life, then you do. When you change your thinking about it, you can change the injury.

The next fight was a big one and Casey really needed to win in order to stay alive. Things fell into such a great routine that I based my future training for MMA athletes on it to help condition themselves. My system worked well and Casey was looking like a top fighter.

And I felt empowered. I'd spent a good portion of my life hiding or getting beat up. Now I was training a top UFC fighter, and preparing to head back to the ring with him.

I felt more alive than I'd felt in years. I'd spent a good part of my life wishing I could just be a part of something, and this was something really, really big!

I savored every second of our training together. When the team got together, I really worked hard to meet everyone's needs, and learn what I could in order to make Casey successful. I tracked everything from the number of reps Casey did to how many calories he ate at a meal. The team knew I was as dedicated as any one of them.

Heck, I didn't even let Casey carry around a light backpack.

We participated in six fights in three years, training every day in between. The last fight against a Japanese opponent, who demonstrated the ultimate samurai warrior spirit, was likely his most challenging to date.

The night before the fight, the whole team went to see the movie "300." I can still hear the music in my head and the emotion from the movie carried over into the next day for all of us. Being behind the scenes at a UFC fight was a marvel, and the only way I can describe it was organized chaos. Again, the atmosphere right before the fight was thick; you could feel the energy just coming off everybody in the room. Casey broke the silence by yelling, "Tonight, we dine in hell!" a line from the movie, and the entire team howled in unison. We knew the line from the movie of the previous night where 300 Spartans fought to the last man against over 200,000 Persians.

The Spartans believed they would triumph.

As a part of Casey's team, I knew we all believed the same.

Three years of work, the last six months the most serious, all led up to this fight.

Goldie, the announcer, noted Casey's change in physique before that huge audience in the Palms Hotel. I knew that was pumping Casey up, like I'd been doing for six months. External validation means a lot. That's something I've learned over the years so to hear it announced over the loudspeaker definitely jazzed me, and I could see Casey get pumped up too.

The bell.

The fight.

Round one.

Round two.

In the third round, Casey faltered from a lack of concentration and I felt a fleeting moment of panic, but I'd trained this fighter. He pulled it out and won the fight!

That moment, I road high on the roar of the crowd in the auditorium, a din so loud I couldn't hear a thing even if I wanted to.

And at that moment, I realized the kid who had always been picked last had been part of something really huge, and I had played an important role in creating it.

All those years of bullying and the pain of my father's death disappeared in a flash.

I was pulled one way then another. Hugs all around. The announcers shouted about Casey's comeback. They shoved me in front of the cameras and I found myself on live TV.

Life is good!

I didn't get here by myself. My wife stayed home with my two little girls so I could come out for this fight. When I realized I couldn't get a cell signal, I grabbed Mark's ring credential so I could go out where it was quieter to make the call.

Our shared excitement and support validated all the hours and hours of hard training. After about ten minutes of talking a mile a minute, I knew I had to get back to the team.

Little did I know while I was gone, Mark had been stopped by security and could not get back ringside because I had his credential pass. He greeted me with teeth bared and a roar of fury that catapulted me from the pinnacle of my life right back to the lowest moments of my days of being bullied.

My hands grew sweaty, then clammy. Mark's words showered over me like bullets, each one nicking, gouging, drawing blood. I feel a sensation I hadn't felt in years, that feeling of abject fear and failure.

I'd worked so hard to overcome my insecurities as a kid, raised myself up to one of the top MMA trainers in the world, and it all disappeared in a flash.

It only took an instant, but I pushed the old me aside, and took a step forward.

"I'm sorry."

I was. It was my fault. I took his pass. I had selfishly disregarded his needs while I saw to my own. I didn't need to go back to that bad place.

This time, while it seemed like I was being bullied, I was the one really at fault; and it was time to man up, which is just what I did.

One of my many MMA fitness training workshops around the world (Can Fit Pro 2014)

It took a while due to emotions running understandably high, but that night we went out for dessert and I realized over my apple pie a la mode that I had arrived.

Never again would I take my value, my worth, from someone else. It resides inside of me.

The moment I had acknowledged it, I felt a warm glow of peace that had been missing from my life for a very long time

Now you have my story.

As you read, even as a well-respected, fight training adult, I instantly felt dehumanized when confronted by Mark for not bringing his credential pass back. His angry words and actions took me instantly back to the days when I had been yelled at and beat up as a kid. But I was able to separate that from my past experiences.

I realized I didn't have to allow bullying to continue to shape me. It no longer controlled me. If I make a mistake now, I own it. If someone unloads on me without a good reason, I calmly stand up for myself.

No one bullies me today.

Even my UFC clients call me Dr. Evil, but it's because they respect what I am able to do for them in terms of training. None of them would ever consider bullying me.

I have a few last words for you if you're being bullied right now. First, tell someone. There are too many laws in place now for schools to ignore bullying, but they have to be told it's going on. Next, tell your parents or other trusted adults and make sure they take you seriously. Finally, discover what it is in you that makes life meaningful for you. I found my way through martial arts, weight training, and fitness. You might find it there as well and the next section is written by my good friend, Stephen Whittier on how to choose a good martial arts school with an anti-bullying component incorporated into their program.

But, if you're not interested in martial arts, find something else. Maybe you're really good at art, music or drama. Get involved in those groups, classes, and clubs. As you become more skilled, your confidence and self-esteem grows, making you a tougher person to bully.

You'll end up spending a lot more time with people you like, rather than the ones you're pretending to like, who turn around to hurt and abuse you. Perhaps you're a computer whiz or absolutely love chess. There are so many classes, clubs, and groups where you will find like-minded people who are more likely to become friends than bullies.

I've learned, since writing this book, that some of the guys who bullied me came from families who were abusive and they lived a life of being bullied at home.

They didn't know anything else.

This doesn't make it right, and doesn't excuse the way they tormented me. It just made me aware that there was a reason behind their behavior and it allowed me to find it in myself to finally forgive all my tormentors.

And it would be completely irresponsible of me to not mention my inappropriate use of alcohol as a way to handle my misery at being bullied. My story of coming home so drunk that I couldn't do my paper route the next day may seem funny, but on a deeper level it is sad and dangerous.

My father died at a young age, likely of an alcohol-related illness. Alcohol was always around when I was growing up. Weekends, holidays, and parties always had plenty of beer flowing.

It's the way things were growing up for me.

What I didn't learn was responsibility in terms of alcohol.

Once I learned that alcohol numbed my pain, I used it, despite my deepening knowledge of health, diet, and fitness. My bully friends sometimes put up with me when I was able to provide them with an easy way to get booze.

But they didn't like me any better.

And the still bullied me.

They just used me to get alcohol.

At first, I put up with it because it felt like they were being nice to me by letting me party with them when I supplied the alcohol. Then, I realized all alcohol did was dull the pain temporarily. Once the effects had passed, my problems were still there, and were often worse than before.

Alcohol does NOT solve your problems. If anything, it makes them worse. It only delays you in taking steps to actually solve your problem.

Numbing your pain does nothing if you don't also take steps to change the situation.

It took me a while, but I finally learned that to handle any difficult problem in life, I had to approach it with a clear head and rational thinking. I often wondered what might have happened if I had been drinking the night I was confronted at the beach. My self-control might have snapped and my life could have looked much darker today.

Instead, I recognized I wanted very different things in my life than the guys who bullied me did.

I was going places.

Most of my bullies were condemned to live their lives within a few short blocks of where we grew up, running for all they're worth like hamsters in cages, but going nowhere.

For those of you who are being bullied, I want you to know something. While it might seem like you're so miserable right now and there's no end in sight, that's not the truth.

Life changes.

People change.

As you grow and mature and begin to be involved in different activities, your world begins to grow beyond what it is today.

As your world grows, you grow, and before you know it, you've moved beyond this dark period in your life.

My friend, Deacon Dave, told me about his daughter who was teased and bullied mercilessly because she was very, very thin. She eventually dropped out of school, despite having changed schools to evade her bullies. Unfortunately, the bullying began almost immediately in the new school and she could not stand it. She dropped out of school at sixteen, but did sit for her GED. In that way, she was able to get away from her bullies and she now has her eye on getting into nursing school.

Sometimes, it just takes just getting into an activity you enjoy; one that builds self-esteem, and helps you to develop friends in those activities, as I did in my martial arts and weight lifting.

Other times, you have to completely change your environment in order to get away from your bullies.

The key is to keep fighting for yourself.

I know, first-hand, how long-lasting the pain and scars of bullying can be.

I carry them with me to this day.

But I've chosen to build a very successful career teaching people how to train for world-class competition and I don't think I would have the same tenacity for it without my past experiences.

My life now is terrific. I have fabulous friends, a lovely wife, and two adorable daughters. I travel the world training people in the ways of fitness and my mission includes talking to people about how to overcome bullying.

My girls, who have learned about bullying too

CHOOSING THE RIGHT MARTIAL ARTS ANTI-BULLYING PROGRAM: AN INSTRUCTOR'S GUIDE FOR PARENTS

By Stephen Whittier, MA
Founder & Chief Instructor
Nexus Martial Arts & Fitness (Wareham, MA)
www.NexusMa.com

As a professional educator and martial arts instructor with a passion for helping kids and teens cultivate higher levels of self-esteem and deal responsibly with bullies, I am used to addressing some common misconceptions on the part of parents.

On one end of the spectrum, some believe that studying martial arts for anti-bullying equates to teaching children how to fight. We have to field this objection on two fronts – both from those who don't want their children to use violence as a solution, as well as from the parents who want their children to take a stand against bullies, even if that means using physical force.

The fact is that while we do teach self-defense, fighting is the absolute last (and least desirable) option on a full menu of conflict-avoidance strategies our students learn. Parents who envision some hard-edged, "no mercy" environment like the nefarious Cobra Kai from *The Karate Kid* will be quite surprised to say the least. Quite frankly, kids who are regularly exposed to our curriculum will be light years ahead of their peers when it comes to managing the social and psychological pressure of bullying if they experience it.

On the other end of the spectrum, we also encounter parents who come to us because they have "heard" that martial arts is good for building confidence, discipline, and helping kids deal with bullying. I consider this a mixed blessing of sorts, because although I'm glad that this impression led them to take action and find my program, I also know the following: martial arts practice in itself does not develop these benefits (at least not in a meaningful or lasting way). The truth is that the effectiveness of each individual program comes down to the curriculum and the knowledge, attitude and training of the instructors.

This is why the child's (and parent's) experience may vary dramatically from one martial arts program to the next. In fact, many instructors operate under the same misconception, thinking that the activity itself is the confidence builder and bully prevention program. But when it comes to the actual "know how" of systematically teaching children to develop the personal resources to deal with bullying, the unfortunate truth is that many haven't a clue.

That said, here's my first recommendation. Do a little research up front and see if the school you're looking at appears to have any expertise in character development and anti-bullying. Ask for referrals from other parents you trust, look at the website or other promotional information to get a sense of the school's identity, and of course, make an appointment so you can evaluate the program firsthand.

My second recommendation may reveal a bit of bias on my part, but it's also something I believe in strongly. This has to do with practicality and authenticity.

Broadly speaking, for all the different martial arts schools and disciplines out there (and there are many), when it comes to the physical skills aspect, they can be divided into two categories: fantasy based and reality based (not to be confused with a training facility that claims to "train for the street"… ironically, these can be the most fantasy-based of all). My preference and recommendation is, if possible, to find a school that trains realistic physical skills.

Make no mistake…just about every type of martial arts program promotes "practical self-defense." And in the minds of most parents who are not familiar with martial arts, it's all just "karate" or "tae kwon do" anyway, and they often see the closest available option as interchangeable with any others. This is completely normal, of course; whenever we are novices in a certain field or industry, we tend to think in terms of generalities, whereas the more knowledgeable we become, the more we're able to think in terms of specifics and identify differences.

There are vast differences in the functionality of various martial arts approaches, just as there are vast differences in the teaching experience of various instructors. Just because we don't promote fighting or talk about it in our regular classes does not mean we should not train our students to be able to perform under real pressure if they were ever faced with an unavoidable physical assault. To that end, as instructors, it is our duty to place objective reality over any emotional investment we have in what we teach or delusional beliefs in its effectiveness.

The point of this is not to enter into a debate over styles. Instead, I prefer to think about functional performance first. With proper training, my students have skills to defend themselves if someone actually grabs or tackles them or tries to assault them with strikes. We know this because our training methods allow them to develop these skills in a safe and progressive manner so they are not theoretical, but tested.

I'm thankful for all the kids we've helped to become more confident and responsibly handle real life bullying situations. Only a handful ever had to use their physical skills to protect themselves. In a couple of situations, however, these situations were serious, and you can bet those students and their parents were very glad they had functional skills at their disposal.

That being said, this approach to developing martial arts skills extends far beyond actual self-defense. It has to do with building an honest sense of self, an authentic confidence based in a child knowing exactly what he or she can and cannot do – as opposed to what they want to think they can do (which would be a fantasy-based sense of confidence). When you combine this level of sincerity with a positive, goal-oriented environment, expertise in character development, and a truly practical curriculum of skill development, you have a recipe for success that holds lifelong benefits for your child.

Giving an "Overcome Bullying" workshop in the U.K.

BURN WITH KEARNS' OVERCOME BULLYING PROGRAM

Looking ahead, what do you want from an anti-bullying program?

Things were a bit different when I went to school. We didn't have laws to protect kids from bullies. Parents and teachers alike believed that all you had to do was stand up for yourself and problem solved.

Most of the time, you were encouraged to either "punch them in the nose" or just ignore them. After all, "boys will be boys" as my mother told me.

I'm living proof that ignoring the problem didn't work.

It still doesn't work today.

Words and actions of harm and exclusion still hurt.

One would think that with all the attention given to the problem of bullying, it would be better for kids, and in some schools, I think it is.

But based on the number of kids I talk to both in the U.S. and abroad, bullying is still one of the biggest problems school children face.

Learning to deal with bullies is a life skill. There are plenty of kids who are bullies all their lives, so you do need to figure out how to deal with them. One of the first things is to realize that while you're in school, you may feel trapped, but please know, it's only temporary.

I totally felt trapped while I went to school.

My neighborhood was my whole world.

Until I learned the world was bigger than my neighborhood, I felt stuck with the same people I'd known all my life. And when my friends turned into enemies, I lived in a war zone. I did everything I could to make my enemy-friends like me again.

But nothing worked.

Until Lionel said it, I didn't ever consider finding new friends.

But that's the basis for change.

If you can't change your environment, change the people you hang out with.

That's one thing within your control.

Get involved with people who like the same things you do.

Martial arts did it for me.

I'm not going to give you a great big, huge anti-bullying program because a single approach doesn't work for everyone. What I will do is give students, parents, and educators some guidelines on how to deal with your current bullying problem.

IMPORTANT FACTS ABOUT BULLYING

64% of children who were bullied did not report it, and 36% did

(Source: Petrosina, Guckenburg, DeVoe, and Hanson)

Bullying is associated with negative consequences that can last far longer than the years a child spends in school; two of those are depression and poor health.

When bullying incidents are not reported, school officials are not able to properly identify the scope or frequency of bullying behavior in their schools. This incomplete picture of bullying further hampers educators' attempts to curtail bullying.

More kids report on bullying when the following incidents are involved:

- Injury
- Physical threats
- Destruction of personal property
- Physical contact like pushing or shoving
- When bullying happens more frequently
- When multiple types of bullying occur
- When bullying happens outside of school
- When bullying happens on a school bus

Fewer reporting results occurred when the following incidents occurred:

- Making fun of the victim occurred
- Name calling
- Excluding the victim from activities
- Spreading rumours about the victim
- Forcing the victim to do things he/she didn't want to do

Many kids don't report bullying because they think they should be able to handle it, or worse, because they've been told by an adult to just "ignore" it and it will stop. In reality, that is far easier said than done.

According to the U.S. Department of Education, these are signs of bullying:

1. Unexplainable injuries
2. Declining grades, not wanting to go to school
3. Difficulty sleeping or frequent nightmares
4. Changes in eating habits
5. Frequent stomachaches, feeling sick, faking illness
6. Sudden loss of friends, avoiding social situations
7. Feelings of helplessness or decreased self-esteem

CYBER BULLYING

Wow, here we have something entirely new since the rise of social media use by school kids. This was something I never had to deal with. I managed to hide in my home, the one safe place in my daily life. With cyberbullying, kids that their bullies follow them to their safest places.

And if you allow it, that's exactly what happens.

What is cyber bullying?

Cyber bullying takes place via smart phones, tablets, computers, and anything that allows students to access their email and social media accounts. It happens when you "friend" someone you want to be friends with. But what happens when your friend turns on you and becomes your enemy? Unless you are strong enough and brave enough to change your privacy settings and learn to block messages from kids who want to hurt you, you will find yourself the target of cyber bullying.

Cyber bullying is a way for bullies to get past parents and educators who might otherwise protect a student. It can become a public forum for humiliation.

One of the worst ways cyber bullying can cause harm is through the use of something called "sexting," which is taking a fairly private selfie and then sending it to someone. Not always a wise idea, but there are now laws that help to protect a victim of cyber bullying in cases of sexting.

The laws do not ban sexting.

A person can share an image of themselves with someone, even if it is a very personal image. So, the laws are not about sharing of images, but they are all about consent or *non-consent* of the sharing of images.

If a girl sends a sexy picture to her boyfriend, he cannot forward things on to his friends unless she gives him permission to do so.

Consent is the key.

How do you prove consent? That's pretty hard. Lack of consent can be assumed. Unless the person posts a picture of themselves publicly on a platform such as Facebook, where the expectation of privacy has disappeared, lack of consent is assumed. There are also further possible charges if the person is under eighteen. But, I don't want to go too much into this.

It's just too bad that we have to have laws to protect people from cyber bullying, or bullying at all.

The key is this:

WORDS HURT!

I don't care if they're said in person, over the phone or over the computer. And cyber bullies are experts at figuring out how to get under your skin. They try to make people feel ashamed, embarrassed, ostracized, unwanted, weird, and unloved.

Serious cases of cyber bullying have led to suicide.

If you don't know how to block someone from your account, ask for help. Tell a parent, guardian, teacher, counselor or even an older sibling. You may even have to go so far as to change your email address. Whatever you have to do to protect yourself, do it. And if you don't know how, get help.

Always, always, always ask for help. Don't assume you have to walk this path alone.

The iSafe Foundation reports that half of teens have experienced some form of cyber bullying online.

How can you not feed in to the trolls who use the internet looking to hurt you?

- Don't respond to negative comments, texts, or emails. That's right, do *not* respond. Bullies feed off your reaction. They *want* you to get upset. This empowers the bully, escalating the situation. Don't forward messages. You have no control over what other people might do with a forwarded message.

- Record and collect evidence. Even if it makes you feel bad to write down what was said and done, keeping detailed records is the best way to stop things. When bullying occurs online, take screenshots of each one with dates and times. Print everything out and then share it with a responsible adult. As I said earlier, it might be a parent, teacher, counselor or even an older sibling. What is important is that you *share* what is happening to you.

- About the responsible adult. I cannot stress this enough. ***Tell someone what is going on.*** Tell your parents, a teacher, the principal at your school or a counselor. Do not try to just deal with this yourself. And if the first people you tell don't think it matters, tell someone else. Keep at it until someone listens and does something to help you. I tried for so many years, but I only shared things with my mother and she didn't know how to help me. Finally, she told my uncle who managed to step in and help me figure out how to deal with my bullying problem. Never feel what bullies tell you is true. You are not responsible for what people say about you and you have every right to expect a responsible adult to help you deal with it.

- Most computers and phones have the capacity to block people from your account. If you get bullying messages on a regular basis, block them! If you have to get your parents involved, do it. All social media sites like Facebook, Instagram, and YouTube make it easy to report harassment.

If necessary, you may need to change phone numbers or create a different email address. If these do not help, have your parents or other responsible adult contact the police because most cyber bullying tactics are against the law.

- Be strong in who you are. This is probably the hardest thing for kids in school to understand, but who you are is the most important thing in the world. Don't change just to please someone else, especially a bully. Find friends who are interested in what you do. Where I found an interest and passion in martial arts, other kids find it in music, science, robotics, theater or art. I tell kids all the time to find their own crew of friends and hang out with them. It took me way too long to figure out I needed some new friends. In fact, Lionel is the one who pointed out to me that my bullies were NOT my friends. I just kept hoping things would change. Don't waste another minute with people who abuse you. And, having a group of friends makes it harder for people to bully you.

SO, WHAT CAN YOU DO ABOUT IT?

Isn't this better phrased as a statement? "What YOU Can Do About It!"

STUDENTS:

There is no one in the world who cares about you more than I do.

Okay, maybe your parents do.

But, I've dedicated the last several years of my life to writing this book and developing the *Overcome Bullying Program* because I care very much about you. I've been where you are and I understand how hard your life is right now. I'm here to tell you, however, that school doesn't last forever, and when you have the ability to expand your world, you have the opportunity to leave your school, your neighborhood, and your bullies behind.

But what do you do until that time?

I've talked to kids who begged their parents to move to a new house. I wished my mom could have moved us, but it was out of the question for me. I told you about the girl who changed schools, but the bullying seemed to follow her. Sometimes you truly are stuck in a situation.

How can you stop being bullied right now?

Today?

Here are the foundational components of my *Overcome Bullying* approach:

- **Speak Up:** Whatever you are going through you need to let others know what is happening. Do *not* keep it to yourself. And if the first person either can't help or doesn't think it's a big enough problem to get involved, ask someone else. Be that squeaky wheel! Make a big deal until you get some attention. Too many kids suffer unnecessarily for far too long. Don't be that kid. Yeah, yeah, I know, the bullies say, "Don't tell or things will get worse." What they *don't* tell you is that if you don't tell, it's going to get worse anyway, because they know you're scared and bullies love that. They love that feeling of power. So whatever you can do to diminish their power will be better for you.

- **Stand Up:** Whether it be physically, mentally, or emotionally, you will eventually need to stand up for yourself. And that takes some courage. You've read my story, so you know how long it took for me to be able to stand up physically to my bullies. And even after I started to stand up for myself, they kept coming after me, but I didn't quit. I kept training, getting stronger, and eventually in my final confrontation, where I knew I could do some serious harm to my bullies, I was ready to fight. But I didn't have to. In that final stand, they knew they no longer had any power over me. I had to make a stand, and I had to do it without going to jail. I don't advocate violence. Ever. But I do advocate learning how to protect and defend yourself. Whatever training you need that gives you the self-confidence to stand up to bullies is worth the time and effort it takes. Anything that makes you physically stronger and more skilled will also give your self-confidence a huge boost. I'm not a very tall guy, but when I became confident in my martial arts training, I felt like I was ten feet tall. And people could tell I was no longer afraid of them.

- **Stay Together:** There is strength in numbers. Bullies don't like a fair fight. They don't like to deal with a group of people. They prefer to pick on a kid or small group of smaller kids because they know they can physically overpower them. You've heard me say, "Get involved in activities that you enjoy and make friends there." When you do that, you suddenly have a group of friends who just might be able to stand up for you, with you or just protect you because now you're part of a group. Bullies do not like to deal with large groups of kids. Their chances of winning go way down. The other important aspect of spending time with people who like to do what you like to do is taking that step to make new friends. I still can't believe how long it took me to finally believe that. Lionel was the first friend who just flat out said it. "You need new friends." It just hadn't occurred to me that I needed to do that. Once

I made the change, my entire life changed because I didn't focus every second of the day on my fear of being bullied. I stopped wondering who was going to pick on me that day and just how I would be humiliated. I began to look forward to activities, spending time with new friends, and before I knew it, my whole outlook on life got brighter. I can't emphasize this step enough!

- **Self Defense:** Self-preservation is a human instinct. This touches on all levels emotionally, physically, and mentally. And the thing about bullying is that it can have long-term effects. So the sooner you learn to defend yourself, the better your life will be in the long-run. When I first started taking martial arts classes, I was a total physical mess. I was picked last for a reason...I was no good at sports. I was small. I was weak. And worst of all, I believed everything my bullies said about me, and that I was worse than having no one on the team. My bullies had me so brain-washed that I totally believed them. But when I entered that dojo, something switched on in my brain, something that made me know my bullies were wrong. Was I a martial arts expert after my first lesson? No way! I still pretty much sucked at every athletic thing I tried. What was different was I no longer believed I had to stay that way. By taking the classes and practicing and practicing and practicing, I could feel my self-esteem grow stronger and stronger. Yes, I still had to deal with the bullies. Remember the counselor who suggested I just use my martial arts training to beat them up? That was his only solution. But by that time, I knew it was the wrong thing to do. I could only use my training in self-defense. I couldn't go out and just pick off my bullies one by one. That was the wrong thing to do. But, by learning self-defense, and understanding when it was OK to use it, I became mentally stronger than my bullies. I can't tell you how great it feels to do something that improves your physical fitness. It doesn't have to be martial arts. It can be dance or track and field. Just do something physical because your brain gets the benefit of endorphins and that make you feel better about yourself. Physical training in anything makes you less of a target for bullies. But I will absolutely advocate for anyone who feels the need to learn some self-defense skills.

Be sure you understand the difference between being bullied and just experiencing rudeness from another person. I never want to diminish anything you experience, but getting hurt, whether physically or emotionally by someone is not always being bullied.

Rudeness is when someone does something inadvertently that hurts someone else. This includes things like someone burping in your face, bragging about getting a better grade or even throwing a snowball in someone's face. How can you tell that it's not bullying? When a kid does something spontaneously, even though it shows poor manners or thoughtlessness, it is not done with a real intent to harm someone.

Even someone "being mean" is not always bullying. This can be saying or doing something to purposefully hurt someone once. This can be motivated by having angry feelings or thinking that if you put someone else down, it will make you look good. Both rudeness and being mean are inappropriate behaviors, they are not considered to be bullying behavior. In the case where I attacked the kid smaller than I was, I felt like I was being a bully. My behavior certainly seemed like it, but I immediately felt remorse, and I never did it again. There was definitely a perceived imbalance of power. I thought I could beat him up. But I never, ever did it again. In that respect, I'm glad to know I wasn't a bully. But I was definitely mean to a smaller kid, and I'll never forget doing that.

Bullying is different. It is an intentional aggressive behavior that happens over and over. It always involves an imbalance of power. Kids who bully say and do things on purpose to hurt another kid, and they keep doing it without every showing signs of remorse. Even when the kid being bullied begged them to stop, they don't. Bullying doesn't always mean physical abuse. It can be verbal, and it can be social where a student is made to feel left out on purpose, ostracized from the group, social exclusion, hazing or even rumor spreading. And now there is cyber bullying.

As hard as it is, try to be sure that when you complain about bullying, it really is bullying behavior. Sometimes it is hard to perceive the difference, so be sure to discuss it with an adult. Sometimes it can really help to have their perspective to help understand the difference between someone being rude and bullying. Rudeness can usually be dismissed in a day or two. Bullying can go on for years and will negatively impact the victim.

PARENTS:

It's such a hard job helping our kids grow into self-reliant individuals. How do you know the difference between being a "helicopter" parent and one who nurtures, empowers, and still allows a child to make mistakes so they can learn from them?

How do you build confidence?

One of the best ways is to take a step back and really observe what is happening to your child. Stress in life can actually be a positive thing. We all have to learn to manage stress because it is pretty much a given in our lives. Bullying experiences can be stressful, and with proper guidance, these can teach your kids to learn how to handle things in the future.

Learn self-defense...anyone, any age. Do it!

My daughter is 11 and she trains

Our kids trust us implicitly. My own kids, I counsel and guide. I help my kids manage what comes down the pike. I help them manage happiness and joy. I help them manage failure and pain. I have to help them manage it all. Learning to do this well comes with time and experience.

If you've never been bullied, you may have trouble helping your child handle their experiences. I mean, how do you explain the concept of "hot" to a child? Until they touch a hot stove and get burned, the concept of "hot" is vague. So is the idea of pain coming from the words or actions of another student, especially if your child used to be friends with that individual.

In my case, my mom and dad really couldn't understand what happened to me when my closest friends turned into enemies. Mom thought that "boys will be boys" and I should just put up with it until it was over. Dad figured, "A good punch in the nose ought to straighten them out." Obviously, my parents either didn't appreciate just how bad things were for me or they felt as helpless as many parents I talk to today.

When it comes to our kids, we hate to see them hurt.

I hate seeing my kids hurt.

So, our job is to help them deal with being bullied. They need to learn how to deal with the emotions they feel that can range from anger and frustration and rage to sadness and depression. What can you do to make sure your kids don't take this negative time in their young live along with them for the rest of their life?

First, when your child comes to you with a report of being bullied, listen carefully. Make sure it really is bullying behavior, and not just someone being rude or periodically mean. There are plenty of mean people in the world. Just watch how people drive on the freeway or in a parking lot after church. But unless they target you every day or every week, that couldn't be construed as bullying behavior. You'll have to teach your kids how to deal with rude and mean people, too.

But bullying behavior is far more damaging. Get on board. Get the educators and counselors at your school on board. And if things escalate to the point you feel helpless, get the authorities on board. Just about every state has laws on the books that deal specifically with ongoing bullying behavior. Your child should never suffer any longer than necessary.

This is not the only thing you can do.

I'm going to tell you that your kid should get involved in physical fitness. I absolutely advocate teaching kids self-defense. But that's not the only purpose for physical fitness. I call exercise the "street sweeper" of negative chemicals that come from a fight or unpleasant encounter with a fellow student. We have receptor sites in our brain, and they need a binding site.

Constant stress is taxing to the adrenals. Physical exercise rejuvenates the adrenals.

And parents, if you're having a stressful time at work, this advice is good for you too.

Stress is good only as long as it stimulates us to perform better.

Constant stress causes mental and physical disease such as depression, diabetes, high blood pressure, depressed immune systems, interrupted sleeping patterns, and more.

We know as adults that ongoing stress is not good for us. It's not good for our kids either.

Exercise is a very inexpensive antidepressant. It makes you feel good immediately, and you feel accomplished.

In my case, my first love is martial arts. Now I'm really digging yoga. At my core, what's there? My training.

Martial arts.

I always go back to martial arts. There I go back to breathing and that feeling of oneness. You always have your breath. They teach that in yoga, in swimming, in running. You always have your breath. When you're breathing, you're alive.

The thing about physical fitness and exercise is you don't have to be good at it to enjoy the benefits of it! If you feel like riding a bike, do it. Feel like a game of tennis or racquet ball? Do it.

Walk around the block.

Jog if you like.

Take a yoga class.

Move and you improve.

Every day you train as an adult, it's like a deposit in your fitness IRA.

Every day you train as kids, you're ensuring longevity for your spirit, your body, and your mind.

See what I did there?

Yeah, I tricked you a little. I got you thinking about yourself, your life, your own physical fitness and stress. I did this because I want you to appreciate how important it is for your kids to overcome any ongoing stress they're experiencing in their lives right now. As I said earlier in this section, if you haven't experienced it, you don't understand it.

While you may have never been bullied, you do understand ongoing and constant stress.

The solution for you and your child can be physical fitness.

Maybe you could even do it together.

Whatever you do, be sure that you listen, really listen to your kids. If they are being bullied, do not wait to act.

As I told the kids, ask for help.

No one should ever go through an experience like this alone.

EDUCATORS:

In addition to everything I've already shared with the students and parents in this section, you have some additional work to do. Let's start with my 4-S approach, outlined above in the students' section. I'm going to give you some additional thoughts for each one.

- **Speak Up:** If a child comes to you to "speak up," I want you to listen. Don't brush them off. Most often, by the time a student brings a report of bullying to you, it's been going on for a long time. And it took a lot of guts and courage for a student to come to you to ask for help. Most kids don't want to make a scene. Most children are told to just "take" it and it will eventually end. But the headlines of newspapers around the country belie that approach. Too many kids have taken their lives as a result of being bullied. Emergency room personnel tell patients all the time, "If you think you're having a heart attack, come in. We'd rather you be wrong and have to send you home than have you die." It's no different with a kid who is really being bullied. So your job is to encourage kids to speak up. There are times when kids will have to break the rules in order to be heard. Don't punish them for it. They wouldn't come to you if they didn't really believe they needed help. And if the situation is not bullying, help them understand that and give them tools to deal with it. Check back with that student to see how things are working out. I'm encouraging students to be a squeaky wheel. Many educators won't appreciate that because it might cause too many false alarms. But I'm right there with the ER folks; I'd rather save the life of one kid than make your lives easier. When enough kids begin speaking up, you'll learn where the problems are in your school and then you can develop programs to address the issues facing your students.

- **Stand Up:** I'm teaching kids to stand their ground. It's your job to give them the tools and the right to stand up to their bullying antagonists. Help them develop the spiritual, emotional, and physical strength to stand up to their bullies. Teach tenacity. Things take time to resolve, and, you don't

Sharing my story as a play in 2015.

want the bullied kids in your office every single day. So give them the tools they need to be able to stand up to their bullies. Teach them how to keep coming back over and over. Sooner or later, bullies back off. This is also where you must advocate for students who are being bullied. Your bullies, and very possibly their parents, will stand their ground and attack you for your position. As educators, you must stand up to the adult bullies who will come to you, threaten you, and bully you to give their child the benefit of the doubt. I would never tell you to falsely accuse anyone of anything, but when a student complains about another student, investigate it. And if you delegate that to another educator, be sure to follow up. Keep notes…very, very detailed notes. Because there are laws now about bullying, you must be sure you have done everything to stand up to the bullies in your school and protect the victims.

- **Stay Together:** Do you have enough additional activities available in your school? This is one of the best ways for bullied students to find their own solution. And if there is a bullying problem with a student, make sure the educator in charge of a particular club or extra-curricular activity is made aware of the situation so they can join your team and advocate for that student. When kids join clubs or activities with other like-minded students, it will make your job easier. They'll stop focusing only on the bully and what happens to them that day. They will also develop greater self-esteem because they're making friends, participating in an enjoyable activity, and developing new skills they can take with them in the future. If your school doesn't have a good variety of activities, this might be a place to start. Get parents and community members involved in this endeavor as well. Rather than seeing it as "someone else's" problem, come together and develop a solution together.

- **Self Defense:** I know. Just about every educator shudders when I suggest self-defense. They protest, "We'll get a lawsuit." But the thing is this key point: Most kids who are getting bullied likely have the right to bring a lawsuit against your school. So you're just fooling yourself in thinking that helping kids learn everything there is to know about self-defense is a liability. By empowering former victims, you will simply diminish your bullying problem. Word gets around schools really fast. Once a bully has been beaten, the whole school knows it. It neutralizes them in many ways. Notice, I said "self-defense" not "learn how to beat up your bullies." Initially, when I started martial arts, that was absolutely the first thing on my mind. But the idea behind martial arts is to defend oneself. Initially, martial arts was developed because they needed to protect their homes, their temples, their followers. They trained because they had to be able to defend, not because they needed to be the aggressors. Martial arts teaches to use only as much force is necessary to neutralize a bully or an aggressor. Not to beat them up. The only time self-defense becomes violent is when the aggressor escalates it. Students will learn to use their minds, asking themselves questions like, "How do I defuse this attack? Do I stare them down? Should I act crazy?" It gives them a lot of tools to constructively use to deal with something that is already in their lives. Self-defense teaches the student control. It teaches to escalate only as much as the situation warrants. You don't have to go from zero to sixty in a split second. Students learn the difference between being uncomfortable and being unsafe.

ADDITIONAL WORK

As I mentioned before, as an educator, you have additional work to do. The biggest thing is to help students learn the concept of empathy. And the younger the student is when you start, the better. Social scientists have suggested that lack of empathy is today's greatest failing in society. Without empathy, students can't appreciate what another student may be going through.

When students feel you care, it's easier for them to treat others kindly. One of the biggest reasons for bullying is that bullies don't feel good about themselves. Most of the bullies in my life were abused at home. That didn't help me much, and, not until I was an adult did I appreciate that fact.

Have classes or sessions where students can actually talk about feelings. When students are able to identify feelings and actually name them, it helps them deal with bullying situations. They can more correctly identify the difference between bullying and rude behavior. Some schools have even set up committees of students to talk about situations and brainstorm about ways to intervene.

Reading books like *To Kill a Mockingbird* helps students understand the goal behind exploring perspectives. Learning to "stand in another man's shoes" for a while helps students appreciate how life might be different for another student. Help students find common ground, it often exists, but both are often too wrapped up in the anger emotions of the bullying situation to be able to do that.

Use whatever techniques are necessary to help students understand how their behavior impacts others. One great exercise is to have them crunch up a pristine piece of paper, and then try to smooth out all the wrinkles. That's the effect of bullying. It leaves permanent marks on the student being bullied. Another parent squeezed the contents of a tube of toothpaste out onto a plate and encouraged the student to put the toothpaste back into the tube. When the student said, "Impossible," the parent then said, "Be care what you say to anyone, because you can never take back anything you've said." These examples of teaching kids how their behavior impacts others helps to battle the behavior of bullying, and curtail the spreading of gossip or rumors.

High emotional intelligence is so much more than simply being nice. Empathic students understand their own feelings enough to understand others, manage their own stressful situations, and how to make decisions about relating to others. Not only will this make your school more peaceful, you're actually preparing your students for future success in life.

Empathy or emotional intelligence is an essential life skill. Research has shown that empathy improves life for students as they build healthy and happy relationships with friends. This will later transition into the work place. As such, it is one of the most important foundations in developing an anti-bullying program in your schools.

PHYSICAL FITNESS AND HEALTH

I've said it before, and I'll say it again here. One of the best ways to counteract bullying is to give your students as many opportunities to become as physically fit as possible. Exercise is almost an immediate mood enhancer, and it works for both the bully and the victim.

What kind of snacks and food do you provide your students?

Sugar is considered by some health professionals as lethal as cocaine. If you wouldn't provide such a drug to your students, perhaps you should consider how much sugar is available on a daily basis at your school in both the meals you provide and the vending machines?

I know you can't cut out the consumption of all snacks that do nothing to properly fuel a young body. But you can make better decisions about what your school supplies and offers. Sometimes all students need is the opportunity to eat better and understand why it's important to their developing bodies.

Do you have food and nutrition classes? Do you have a school or community garden? Do you encourage your students to spend time preparing food in the school kitchen? What we put into our bodies is both food and medicine. Far too many students have no idea where their food comes from, and why they should be making different food choices than they do.

This might seem to have nothing to do with a bullying problem in our schools, but it actually does. Research shows that when children

Show up in your life. Surprise your bullies. I did.

are put on a healthy diet of fresh fruits, , and proteins, eliminating sugar, unhealthy fats, and most preservatives results in radically improving many of their learning and social aggression problems.

Serving ready-made food might seem to be an easy path, but when you look at the overall behavior problems in your school, you might see it is merely false economy.

What makes me different than other people? I know that I just stuck to it. I persevered with both my vision and my passion until I reach whatever goal I was looking to reach. There is no better example for students than to give them an example to follow. Make sure your school does what it says it does. Nothing alienates a kid more than to say one thing and do another.

If you take sugar and preservatives off the menu in the lunch room, don't walk around munching on a candy bar in front of the students. If you advocate physical fitness, let the students see all the educators participating in ways that are appropriate for them. If you want them to use empathy in their dealings with bullies, be sure that everyone on your staff models that behavior.

Our kids are our future.

Let's make it a more peaceful and pleasant world for all of us.

TESTIMONIALS AND ENDORSEMENTS

THE WHITE HOUSE

March 4, 2014

Kevin Kearns
Norfolk, Massachusetts

Dear Kevin:

Thank you for the book. I have heard from many individuals
and families from around the world about their unique and shared
experiences, the obstacles they face, and the dreams they are
striving to fulfill. These personal journeys of courage are an
inspiration, and I appreciate you sharing your story with me.

Again, thank you for the book. I wish you all the best.

Sincerely,

Michelle Obama

Michelle Obama likes what I'm doing with my book and my "Overcome Bullying"
workshops and efforts.

Nunthorpe
Academy

Recommendation for Coach Kevin Kearns

Coach Kearns visited our academy along with Shihan Scott O'Keefe in the early part of the autumn term; the visit coincided with the beginning of the last year of compulsory education for our Year 11 students and their preparations for their final exams in the summer of 2015.

Coach led an inspirational assembly for our 275 Year 11 students and, as I have found in all of my interactions with him, spoke with true passion and real enthusiasm. Coach Kearns used numerous of his past experiences to illustrate very simple but powerful messages about goal setting, commitment and resilience; qualities and skills our 15 and 16 year olds need in abundance in this crucial year and beyond.

The tone of the assembly effectively complimented our key messages to our students and was delivered in Coach's unique and inimitable style. Such was the success of his talk that we have invited Coach back to our academy when he next visits the UK in March and also hope to enable him to share his message with several of our partner schools and academies.

I would highly recommend Coach Kearns and am confident that all young people, irrespective of age or background would value the opportunity of listening to him speak.

Danny Yates

Vice – Principal (Curriculum & Achievement)

Nunthorpe Academy
Guisborough Road
Nunthorpe
Middlesbrough
TS7 0LA

Phone **01642 310561**
Fax 01642 325672
Web **www.nunthorpe.co.uk**

Principal: Lee Brown
Company No. 8188507 VAT Registration 142671814

Myton Park
Primary School

Blair Avenue
INGLEBY BARWICK
TS17 5BL
Tel Number 01642 754658
Fax Number 01642 750717
Email: mytonpark@sbcschools.org.uk
Web: www.sbcschools.org.uk/mytonpark

Head Teacher: Mrs Elisabeth Lee

Recommendation for Coach Kevin

Coach visited our school and spoke to all of the children about how to believe in themselves and how to stand up to bullies.

He spoke with real passion and enthusiasm. He had all of the children hooked! He uses real life examples that the children can relate to and quickly gets them involved through interactive responses and questioning. His message is simple – easily recalled with simple language the children can remember and use to their advantage.

The children talked about him for many months after his visit and we still refer to some of his messages when talking to children in school when they are experiencing difficulties.

I would highly recommend him. He has the knack of engaging the children with his very genuine and caring approach.

Elisabeth Lee

Safeguarding is our priority and all staff at Myton Park Primary School are committed to keeping your child safe

8/3/2016

To

Kevin Kearns
Burn with Kearns
Kids Growing Up Strong
940 High St #302
Westwood, MA 02090

Kevin Kearns is a local and national leader who I contracted to work with my Cadets in July
of 2016. L.E.A.P. Cadets is a program for students ages 12-18 who are interested in law
enforcement, military, or emergency services. I asked Kevin if he would be interested in
working with the Cadets, teaching them defensive tactics. Kevin jumped at the opportunity
to help, saying, "tell me where and when!" He arrived with the same enthusiasm he had
on the phone, and provided a high energy two-hour class for the Cadets. Kevin's style
provides more than self-defense tactics; he offers life lessons in confidence and personal
responsibility. One of our Cadets was so impressed by Kevin, he personally reached out
to him for further advice. Kevin was kind of enough to make the connection with this young
student, and even sent him copies of his book "Always Picked Last." The most important
aspect of the L.E.A.P. Program is connection with kids, and Kevin did this with such ease. I
was so impressed and grateful for this most unexpected outcome.

Kevin has also been instrumental with regards to my work with kids in the areas of personal
protection. L.E.A.P. strives to offer real-life (scenario based) self-defense techniques in
each of our programs. As a consultant, Kevin is able to bring his years of experience in
worldwide martial arts training, and provide valuable information as to "what works." He has
certainly become an invaluable resource.

Kevin, thank you for your strong work, kindness, and willingness to help kids! You embody
all of the L.E.A.P. values, and more!

Michelle Palladini
L.E.A.P Program Founder/CEO
Detective/School Resource Officer: Norfolk Police Department
Michelle.palladini@leapprogram.net

L.E.A.P. PROGRAM

508-509-0285
7 Mulberry Lane
Franklin, MA 02038 www.leapprogram.net
michelle.palladini@leapprogram.net

ADDITIONAL RESOURCES

Cohen-Posey, Kate. *How to Handle Bullies, Teasers, and Other Meanies: A Book That Takes the Nuisance out of Name Calling and Other Nonsense.* Highland City, FL: Rainbow, 1995. Print.

Coloroso, Barbara. *The Bully, the Bullied, and the Bystander: From Preschool to High School: How Parents and Teachers Can Help Break the Cycle of Violence.* New York: HarperResource, 2003. Print.

Fitzell, Susan Gingras. *Free the Children!: Conflict Education for Strong Peaceful Minds.* Gabriola Island, BC: New Society, 1997. Print.

Freedman, Judy S. *Easing the Teasing: Helping Your Child Cope with Name-calling, Ridicule, and Verbal Bullying.* Chicago: Contemporary, 2002. Print.

Giannetti, Charlene C., and Margaret Sagarese. *Cliques: 8 Steps to Help Your Child Survive the Social Jungle.* New York: Broadway, 2001. Print.

Kaufman, Gershen, Lev Raphael, and Pamela Espeland. *Stick up for Yourself!: Every Kid's Guide to Personal Power and Positive Self-esteem.* Minneapolis, MN: Free Spirit Pub., 1999. Print.

Olweus, Dan, and Peter Mortimore. *Bullying at School: What We Know and What We Can Do.* Massachusetts: Blackwell, 1994. Print.

Thompson, Michael, Catherine O'Neill Grace, and Lawrence J. Cohen. *Best Friends, Worst Enemies: Understanding the Social Lives of Children.* New York: Ballantine, 2001. Print.

Thompson, Michael, Lawrence J. Cohen, and Catherine O'Neill Grace. *Mom, They're Teasing Me: Helping Your Child Solve Social Problems.* New York: Ballantine, 2002. Print.

ABOUT THE AUTHOR

Boston-based Kevin Kearns is one of the leading strength and conditioning experts in the United States. His work with combat sports athletes is second to none, having helped condition no fewer than 15 UFC fighters by utilizing hi 25 years of martial arts training. His MMA conditioning DVD series remains a best seller, while his "Burn with Kearns" philosophy has gone global with certification events currently being staged around the world.

Having been bullied as a kid, Kevin understands how powerful and long-lasting the pain of bullying can be. By sharing his story, Kevin provides hope to all children who suffer at the hands of a bully. For Kevin, martial arts became his way out. For any one of you, it will be something that is important to you. Pursue your dreams and passions and find other like-minded people to share them with.

Follow your path.

Trust in yourself.

Some of the tools of my trade